SMOKE SIGNALS

introduction, screenplay, and notes by

SHERMAN ALEXIE

SMOKE SIGNALS

HYPERION
new york

All photos by Courtnay Duchin and Jill Sabella

Library of Congress Cataloging-in-Publication Data

Alexie, Sherman

Smoke signals / Sherman Alexie.

p.   cm.

ISBN 0-7868-8392-8

I. Smoke signals (Motion picture)   II. Title.

PN1997.S6115   1998

791.43'72—dc21   98–21018

CIP

Book Design by Kathy Kikkert

FIRST EDITION

10   9   8   7   6   5   4   3   2

to David Skinner, for his faith

to Brian Berdan, for his magic

to all of our fathers,

here and gone

INTRODUCTION

I love movies.

Okay, maybe that's not the most original way to begin an essay about the making of one particular movie. But, I mean it, I really love movies. I always have. I love movies more than I love books, and believe me, I love books more than I love every human being, except the dozen or so people in my life who love movies and books just as much as I do.

Let me explain this in economic terms.

When I was ten years old, my family spent one thousand dollars for a VCR, a video cassette recorder.

Yes, we paid one thousand dollars for a VCR that would probably cost one hundred dollars now. But we bought our VCR in its infancy, when Beta and VHS were both hoping to win the hearts of cinephiles everywhere.

One thousand dollars.

That was more money than my mother and father made as income during a good month. A good two months, in some years.

As a child, a thousand dollars and a million dollars meant the same thing to me: unattainable riches.

Yes, we were that poor, living in reservation poverty, which is like living in the basement of the skyscraper called poverty.

And yet, we paid one thousand dollars for a VCR.

Why?

Because my family, collectively and individually, loved movies.

I was six years old when I first saw *The Texas Chainsaw Massacre*. Or I should say, I was six years old when I first *heard The Texas Chainsaw Massacre*.

It was at the East Sprague Drive-in Theater in Spokane, Washington.

My mother and father were in the front seat of the car while I was pretending to be asleep in the backseat of the car.

I mean, I could have sat up front with my parents and watched the movie. They would not have objected.

You see, Indian parents tend to treat their children as adults. At any kind of Indian gathering—a powwow, a basketball tournament, a ceremony—a dozen Indian kids will roam unsupervised at all hours of the night. Some might think this is a passive form of child abuse, but it really is just a matter of respect and expectation.

My parents would have respected my decision to watch *The Texas Chainsaw Massacre*, but they would also have expected me to handle it with the appropriate maturity.

In other words, any resulting nightmares would have been my own responsibility. At least, my parents would have told me the nightmares were my responsibility as they let me climb into the safety of their bed after the latest such nightmare.

However, since I chose not to watch the movie, my parents respected that decision and expected me to fall asleep in the backseat.

But I could not fall asleep. I was too fascinated by the sound of dialogue, laughter, music, and buzzing chain saws. I was terrified, of course, and would have nightmares for a few weeks afterward. But I also had this need, this burning desire, to sneak peeks at the screen.

Yes, when the buzzing chain saws were at their loudest, I would peer over the front seat, between my parents' heads, and catch brief glimpses of the incredible violence.

Why?

Because I knew there was a great movie going on and I was missing half of it.

An important note: the salesman who sold us our first VCR was a genius.

"Listen, folks," he said. "Go with VHS. Trust me. Beta just ain't going to make it."

I was on the set of *Smoke Signals* on the first day of filming. It was a cold, rainy morning in northern Idaho, meaning it was colder and rainier than anywhere else on the planet.

We were shooting a scene with our young actors, Cody Lightning and Simon Baker.

Both boys were very nervous and were stumbling a bit over some difficult dialogue.

They were beautiful.

My mom was there as well. And she was crying because she thought Simon, all dressed up in suit and glasses, looked just like me at the same age. We looked nothing alike, but I didn't contradict my mother.

Nostalgia can be quite lovely.

One of our adult actors, Gary Farmer, was yelling at the various members of the crew and chastising them for imagined slights and mistakes.

Why was Gary yelling?

I think he was getting into character as the loud, abusive Arnold Joseph.

So I went into the makeup room and yelled at him for yelling. And because I wanted to help him get into character.

During one of the later test screenings of the film, an audience member remarked that she thought Gary Farmer was a national treasure.

It's true.

My dad was there watching us film.

We were filming in DeSmet, Idaho, the small town on the reservation where my father was born.

Yes, a few feet away from the exact spot where my father was born.

I watched the crew set up lights.

My brothers and sisters were drinking coffee a few feet away from the lights.

I watched the producers huddle together.

My brothers and sisters huddled together in a van to take a break from the cold.

I saw the breath of our young actors as they spoke into the cold air.

My brother and sisters talked about all of the movies they loved.

I knew that no matter what else happened during the making of *Smoke Signals*, I was going to make movies for the rest of my life.

I used to think that movies were real.

I mean, I thought, I truly believed, that every movie was actually a documentary.

I believed this long past the age when it could be considered cute.

Once, in Spokane, Washington, when I was eleven years old, an older, larger white kid called me a "dirty fucking Indian."

And I jumped on him, despite his size, fully expecting to be rescued by Billy Jack, the half-breed Indian and Vietnam War veteran portrayed by Tom Laughlin in a series of pulp movies.

My favorite films: *Midnight Cowboy*, *The Graduate*, and *Aliens*.

After we screened *Smoke Signals* in Seattle, I walked down the aisle to field questions from the audience.

As I neared the front of the theater, my big brother leapt to his feet and hugged me. He lifted me off the ground and hugged me until I could barely breathe.

My brother has hugged me twice.

Once, when I hit two free throws to win a big basketball game in high school.

And now, for the second time, when I helped make the movie that made him cry.

Of course, my big brother, tough as he pretends to be, cries at nearly every movie.

An Officer and a Gentleman, *Old Yeller*, *Titanic*, *Police Academy*.

My brother cried at the end of all of those movies and more.

There is one man, a white man, who believed so much in this film by and about Indians, that he completely financed it.

Amazing.

When people ask me, and they do ask me, how I feel about making the difficult transition from writing novels to writing screenplays, I am not always sure what to say.

I mean, screenplays are more like poetry than like fiction. Screenplays rely on imagery to carry the narrative, rather than the other way around. And screenplays have form. Like sonnets, actually. Just as there are expectations of form, meter, and rhyme in a sonnet, there are the same kinds of expectations for screenplays.

Of course, free verse poetry subverts all expectations of formalist poetry.

So, I wonder aloud, who is writing the free verse screenplays?

Once, after watching three or four Bruce Lee movies in a row with my father, I turned to him.

"Dad, " I said. "Do you think Bruce Lee is the toughest fighter in the world?"

"I don't know," he said. "There's probably some guy living in a one-room apartment in some downtown hotel in some stinky city, cooking and eating from a hot plate, while taking a shit and showering in the bathroom at the end of the hall, who is really the toughest fighter in the world."

"Dad," I said. "If Bruce Lee got into a fight with that guy, I'd pay to watch it."

A reminder: *Smoke Signals* is the first feature film written, directed, and co-produced by Indians to ever receive a major distribution deal.

There have been many other Indian filmmakers, our elders, who made wonderful films that have been wrongfully ignored or dismissed.

Our film would not have been possible without the filmmaking efforts of previous generations of Indian writers, directors, producers, and actors.

Since filmmaking is a collaborative sport, sort of like baseball, I'd like to introduce you to the *Smoke Signals* team:

Owner: Harvey Weinstein
Manager: David Skinner
Catcher: Larry Estes
Pitcher: Chris Eyre
First Base: Scott Rosenfelt
Second Base: Brian Capener
Shortstop: Janet Fries Eckholm
Third Base: BC Smith
Left Field: The Crew
Center Field: The Cast
Right Field: Roger Baerwolf
Relief Pitcher: Brian Berdan

But wait, you ask, what about the screenplay, what about the screenwriter? Doesn't he get a chance to play?

Ladies and gentlemen, the screenplay is the *ball*.

SCREENPLAY

We HEAR *the last few moments of an instrumental synthesized disco dance song and the first few words of a female disc jockey.*

FEMALE DISC JOCKEY

(*V.O.*)
Good morning to all you insomniac disco lovers out there. It's 2:45 a.m. on a hot Bicentennial Fourth of July in 1976. I hope you're all curled up with a patriotic lover. I'm sending this next song out to all of you. And just remember, sweethearts, when you get that disco fever, it burns.

◆ **FADE IN:**

1 ◆ EXT. HOUSE—NIGHT

We are looking into a pitch-dark room through an open doorway.

We can only SEE shadows of shadows.

But then a flicker of flames, just a spark, and then the fire begins to grow.

As the flames grow, CAMERA PULLS AWAY and reveals more and more of house.

2 ◆ EXT. DIRT ROAD—NIGHT

CLOSE ANGLE ON ARNOLD JOSEPH, a large Coeur d'Alene Indian man in his thirties.

He is watching the house burn.

His face is illuminated by flames.

He is silent and still for a moment, then makes his decision and runs toward the burning house.

3 ✦ EXT. DIRT ROAD—NIGHT

CAMERA FOLLOWS Arnold Joseph as he is running down a dirt road toward the house that is now engulfed by flames.

We also SEE for the first time other INDIANS stumbling around the burning house.

They are coughing, crying, and screaming.

4 ✦ EXT. BURNING HOUSE—NIGHT

Arnold runs up to the burning house.

INDIANS are stumbling around the house.

They are coughing and gagging from the smoke.

Arnold stops a COUGHING INDIAN MAN.

> ### ARNOLD JOSEPH
> Where's Arlene? Where's Arlene? Where's my wife?

The coughing Indian man cannot speak. He shakes his head and runs away.

ANGLE ON Arnold trying to get in the front door, but the flames and smoke drive him back.

ARLENE JOSEPH is carrying the BABY VICTOR JOSEPH, just a few months old, in her arms when she stumbles up to Arnold.

She had already exited the house.

> ### ARNOLD JOSEPH
> Arlene, are you okay? Are you okay?

> ### ARLENE JOSEPH
> There are people still in there!

We HEAR a scream coming from inside the house.

There is no way Arnold can make it into the house.

ANGLE ON Arnold Joseph as he runs around the house looking for a way to get inside.

ARNOLD'S POV on a pair of hands hanging outside a second-story window.

The hands hold a baby.

The baby is quiet.

The hands thrust the baby upward into the sky.

The baby is BABY THOMAS BUILDS-THE-FIRE, also just a few months old.

Baby Thomas, wrapped in a blanket, is drifting freely upward toward the night stars . . .

Arnold Joseph looks up, his eyes widen, his mouth falls open . . .

Arnold runs across the wet grass, slipping and sliding . . .

Arnold running, his hands outstretched as if he were trying to catch a football . . .

Baby Thomas falling, blanket on fire now, with the burning house behind him . . .

The crowd of Indians, their heads turning to follow Arnold's race to catch Baby Thomas . . .

Arnold diving to make the catch . . .

Baby Thomas hits Arnold's hands and falls through . . .

The crowd of Indians staring with flames dancing on their faces . . .

Arnold stands with Baby Thomas, rips the smoldering blanket off his little body . . .

Arnold stares down at Baby Thomas . . .

ARNOLD'S POV down on Baby Thomas, who is oddly conscious and silent, staring back at Arnold.

5 ✦ INT. BURNING HOUSE—NIGHT

CLOSE ANGLE ON the radio as the flames engulf it.

We HEAR the music crackle and fade out under the weight and heat of the flames.

6 ✦ EXT. BURNED HOUSE—MORNING

The house has burned down to its frame.

Arnold and Arlene Joseph are standing beside each other.

Arnold still holds Baby Thomas.

Arlene holds Baby Victor.

ANGLE ON GRANDMA BUILDS-THE-FIRE, *an Indian woman in her fifties,
as she comes running up to Arnold.*

> **GRANDMA**
> Arnold, what happened? What happened?

Arnold hands Baby Thomas over to his grandmother.

Grandma looks down at her grandson.

> **GRANDMA**
> (cont'd)
> Where's his mother? And father?

Arnold doesn't know what to say. He looks back toward the burned-out house.

Grandma understands. She wails. She brings down the sky with her grief.

7 ✦ EXT. BURNED HOUSE—MORNING

A few hours have passed.

People are sifting through the ashes.

We SEE white sheets over two bodies.

There is now only smoke and grief.

Grandma Builds-the-Fire, still weeping a little, is rocking Baby Thomas.

Arlene, holding Baby Victor, is standing near her.

Arnold stands between Grandma and Arlene.

*ANGLE ON Grandma, with Baby Thomas in her arms, as she looks at Arnold, then
at Arlene and Baby Victor.*

> **GRANDMA**
> (to Arlene)
> Arlene, your son? His name is Victor, enit?

ARLENE JOSEPH

Yes, it is.

GRANDMA

A good name. It means he's going to win, enit?

ARLENE JOSEPH

(to Grandma)
I guess. And your grandson's name is Thomas, enit? What
does it mean?

GRANDMA

I don't know.

Grandma turns her attention to Arnold.

GRANDMA

(to Arnold)
You saved my grandson's life.

ARNOLD JOSEPH

It was nothing. I didn't even think about it . . . I just . . .

GRANDMA

(firmly)
You saved him. You saved Thomas. You did a good thing.

ARNOLD JOSEPH

I didn't mean to.

ANGLE ON Grandma Builds-the-Fire holding Baby Thomas on the left side of FRAME and Arlene holding Baby Victor on the right side of FRAME with Arnold standing between them.

AN INDIAN FIREFIGHTER races between the CAMERA and the Josephs and Builds-the-Fires for a:

SWIPE CUT TO:

8 ✦ EXT. BASEBALL DIAMOND (1988)—DAY

ANGLE ON YOUNG THOMAS BUILDS-THE-FIRE, twelve years old, standing on the left side of the FRAME and YOUNG VICTOR JOSEPH, twelve years old, standing on the right side of the FRAME with a burning barrel sitting between them.

Young Thomas is wearing a thirdhand sport coat with blue jeans and T-shirt.

He also wears very traditionally braided hair and thick glasses.

He is very much an Indian nerd.

Young Victor is wearing a red T-shirt and blue jeans.

He is a very handsome and confident boy.

YOUNG THOMAS
Hey, Victor, what do you know about fire?

YOUNG VICTOR
Thomas, I don't know what you're talking about.

YOUNG THOMAS
No, really, Victor. I mean, did you know that things burn

in colors? I mean, sodium burns yellow and carbon burns orange. Just like that. You can tell what's in a fire by the color of the flames.
(beat)
Hey, Victor, I heard your dad is living in Phoenix, Arizona, now.

YOUNG VICTOR
Yeah, Thomas, what about it?

YOUNG THOMAS
Man, he's lived everywhere since he left you, huh?

Victor ignores Thomas.

YOUNG THOMAS
(cont'd)
I mean, he lived in Neah Bay, and then in Eureka, and then in Riverside, and then in Tijuana, and now in Phoenix, Arizona.
(beat)
Man, Phoenix is like a million miles away from here, enit?

YOUNG VICTOR

Is that so, Thomas?
(beat)
You know, I was wondering. What color do you think your mom and dad were when they burned up?

Young Thomas is hurt by this. He is silent for a moment.

YOUNG THOMAS

You know, your dad ain't coming back.

YOUNG VICTOR

Yes, he is.

YOUNG THOMAS

No, he's gone. When Indians go away, they don't come back. Last of the Mohicans, last of the Sioux, last of the Navajo. last of the Winnebago, last of the Coeur d'Alene people . . .

YOUNG VICTOR

(interrupting Thomas)
Shut up, Thomas. Or I'll beat you up again.

Long beat.

YOUNG THOMAS

What does it mean?

YOUNG VICTOR

What does what mean?

YOUNG THOMAS

What does Phoenix, Arizona, mean?

CUT TO:

OPENING CREDITS ROLL

CUT TO:

CUT TO:

9 ✦ EXT. SILVER MOBILE HOME—DAY

ANGLE ON a shiny silver mobile home sitting quietly beside a dirt road.

This is Arnold Joseph's Phoenix home.

A small white dog lies in the dirt in front of the trailer.

A makeshift basketball hoop and backboard are nailed to a post that is in turn sunk into the ground.

A worn, incredibly battered yellow pickup truck sits beside the trailer.

Beneath the burning Arizona sun, the trailer seems to be very isolated in this lunar landscape of red dust and red rock.

WIDE ANGLE ON the same silver mobile home, but now we can also SEE another more contemporary trailer home sitting a short distance farther down the dirt road.

It is fairly small.

We then SEE a blue car approaching on the road.

As the car draws closer, we HEAR the white dog begin to howl.

ANGLE ON SUZY SONG, an Indian woman in her mid-twenties, who is driving the car.

She is wearing a nice business suit.

She has long black hair, brown skin and eyes, and is very attractive.

She is singing along to a song on the car radio.

WIDE ANGLE ON Suzy's car as it pulls up in front of her trailer.

Her car is much nicer than her small trailer.

She steps out of the car, stops briefly as she hears the do[g]

She listens for a moment then opens her car trunk and p

She has obviously been on a vacation or business trip

She lifts the suitcase and a laptop computer bag out of the trunk and sets them on ...
ground.

The dog continues to howl.

Suzy listens for a moment and then walks toward Arnold Joseph's trailer.

ANGLE ON Suzy as she is walking.

> **SUZY SONG**
> (to dog)
> Kafka? Hey, Kafka? What's the matter, boy?

ANGLE ON Suzy as she kneels down beside Kafka, the white dog, who is now whimpering.

She pets him but he doesn't respond.

> **SUZY SONG**
> What is it, boy? Where's your master, huh? Where's Arnold?

ANGLE ON Suzy as she walks toward Arnold's trailer.

She picks up a basketball and shoots at the outdoor hoop.

She MISSES the shot.

As she walks toward Arnold's trailer, she smells something terrible.

She covers her mouth and nose with one hand.

She tries to open the front door of the trailer, but it is locked.

...ks around the side of the trailer to the kitchen window.

✦ INT. SILVER MOBILE HOME—DAY

CAMERA POV out the trailer's kitchen window as we see Suzy looking inside.

Throughout Arnold's trailer, we SEE that maps and travel posters cover the walls.

There is a bare amount of furniture and an old-fashioned turntable and albums in the living room.

There is a table and chairs in the kitchen, along with a couple sets of plates and glasses.

The bedroom and bathroom are clean and mostly bare.

Other than that, there is a conspicuous lack of possessions, as if Arnold had just moved in, even though he'd been there for years.

FROM CAMERA POV, Suzy disappears from kitchen window and CAMERA MOVES through trailer to living room window, where Suzy appears, peering inside.

She disappears from living room window. CAMERA MOVES back through trailer, down hallway into bathroom, and to the window.

Suzy is peering through the bathroom window.

She disappears from bathroom window.

CAMERA MOVES away from bathroom window, out of bathroom, down the hall toward the bedroom, then into bedroom.

We SEE a body, obviously dead and very decomposed, lying facedown on the bed.

This is Arnold Joseph.

He is wearing only a pair of boxer shorts.

We SEE that a red shirt and a pair of blue jeans are draped over a chair.

Black boots on the floor.

CAMERA MOVES across bedroom to a CLOSE ANGLE on a blank television set.

CAMERA MOVES UP to empty window above television.

The window is empty for a beat, then Suzy's face appears.

She peers in, sees what is inside.

Shock on her face, then pain and grief, horror.

She disappears from the window.

CUT TO:

✦ TITLE CARD: ''COEUR D'ALENE INDIAN
RESERVATION, IDAHO, 1998''

CUT TO:

11 ✦ EXT. ISOLATED LANDSCAPE—COEUR D'ALENE
RESERVATION—DAY

WIDE ANGLE ON a basketball hoop and half-court set in the middle of an isolated landscape, a flat valley surrounded by pine trees and rolling hills.

Very green and beautiful.

We can also SEE THREE INDIAN MEN playing basketball.

The basket clearly does not belong in such a beautiful and remote place, but there it is.

CAMERA MOVES in on the basketball court and we can more clearly SEE that two of the Indian men, JUNIOR and BOO, are wearing white T-shirts and black shorts while the third, the ADULT VICTOR JOSEPH, twenty-two years old, wears a bright red T-shirt and cutoff blue jeans.

We can HEAR the sounds of their exertion: grunting, heavy breathing, squeaking of basketball shoes on the cement, ball bouncing, curses.

CAMERA MOVES closer and closer to the players, onto the court itself, until we are in the middle of their game.

The game is very loud and passionate now.

We HEAR shouts of encouragement, insults, curses, etc.

We continue to HEAR the basketball players as the CAMERA MOVES through the game, off the court on the opposite side, leaving the court behind.

At this point, we notice, in the distance, a LONE FIGURE walking toward the game.

We also notice that this lone figure, who is the ADULT THOMAS BUILDS-THE-FIRE, twenty-two years old, is engaged in some sort of mysteriously repetitive behavior as he walks toward the court.

Thomas is a short, slight Indian man with very traditional braids.

He wears a three-piece suit and tennis shoes.

He is constantly smiling.

As the CAMERA MOVES closer and closer to Thomas, we begin to understand what he is doing.

As he walks toward the game, Thomas is transporting, in an assembly line fashion, a plastic chair, a small end table, and a portable radio.

He has all three items set in a line: the radio in front, then the end table, and the chair at the rear.

Thomas picks up the last item in line, the chair, walks it to the front and sets it down.

Then he walks to the back of the line and picks up the end table, walks to the front of the line, and sets it in front of the chair.

Then he walks to the back of the line, picks up the radio, and then walks to the front of the line again and sets it down in front of the end table.

He repeats this process again and again, making sure, steady, and slightly crazy progress toward the court.

The CAMERA MOVES BACKWARD away from Thomas, onto the basketball court, through the middle of the game again, and just off the court, where it STOPS for a:

WIDE ANGLE ON the basketball court, as Victor Joseph, who is obviously the most talented player on the court, scores at will and plays tenacious defense.

Victor has long, black, unbraided hair. He is a tall, very handsome man.

As the following exchange happens, we SEE Thomas, in the background, as he finally arrives at courtside.

He sets his chair and end table closer to one another, and then sets his radio on the end table.

He fiddles with the dials trying to find a signal.

> **VICTOR**
> *(to Junior, who is guarding him)*
> Game point, cousin, game point.

> **JUNIOR POLATKIN**
> Bring it on, Victor, bring it on.

Junior Polatkin smiles at Victor, who is completely serious.

Victor fakes left, drives right, hesitates, then spins around Junior and Boo for the winning lay-in, which Victor somehow misses.

> **VICTOR**
> Foul!

Junior picks up the loose ball, advances on Victor.

> **JUNIOR POLATKIN**
> Bullshit! There wasn't no one near you, Victor!

> **VICTOR**
> *(taking the ball from Junior)*
> If I say it's a foul, then it's a foul.

Junior knocks the ball away from Victor.

It bounces off the court and rolls to a stop at Thomas's feet.

Thomas looks down at it as if it were a dead animal.

> **VICTOR**
> Hey, Thomas, give us some help, huh?

Thomas hesitates, but then picks up the basketball, and throws it weakly back toward Victor.

Thomas is extremely clumsy and awkward, so the ball only makes it halfway to Victor.

Victor looks at the other players, who are laughing at Thomas's weakness.

Victor walks over to the ball, picks it up, and looks at Thomas.

Thomas is embarrassed and intimidated by Victor.

> **VICTOR**
> (shaking his head)
> Nice suit, Thomas.

Laughing, Victor turns back to his game.

As he dribbles the ball into play, the CAMERA MOVES above the court, focuses on the wooden basketball backboard, which has a bright red sun painted on it.

MATCH DISSOLVE TO:

12 ✦ EXT. SILVER MOBILE HOME—PHOENIX, ARIZONA—DAY

ANGLE ON the flashing red lights of a police car.

WIDE ANGLE ON the police car and an ambulance parked in front of the silver mobile home.

Suzy Song, still wearing her nice business suit, is talking to a WHITE POLICEMAN, who is taking notes.

TWO WHITE AMBULANCE MEN, wearing surgical masks against the smell, carry Arnold Joseph's body out of the trailer.

> **SUZY SONG**
> His name is Arnold Joseph.

13 ✦ EXT. BASKETBALL COURT—COEUR D'ALENE RESERVATION—DAY

ANGLE ON Victor Joseph and his basketball buddies, Junior and Boo, as they sit on the court.

In the background we SEE Thomas is still sitting with his radio, chair, and little plastic table.

> **JUNIOR POLATKIN**
> Hey, Victor, who do you think is the best basketball player ever?

> **VICTOR**
> That's easy. Geronimo.

> **JUNIOR POLATKIN**
> Geronimo? He couldn't play basketball, man. He was Apache, man. Those suckers are about three feet tall.

> **VICTOR**
> It's Geronimo, man. He was lean, mean, and bloody. Would have dunked on your flat Indian ass and then cut it off.

> **JUNIOR POLATKIN**
> Yeah, sometimes it's a good day to die. Sometimes, it's a good day to play basketball.

> **BOO**
> What about Sitting Bull?

> **VICTOR**
> A veteran player. Would have used those old-man moves. Stepping on your foot so you can't jump. Holding your

shirt when you tried to run by him. Poke you in the belly
when you take a shot.

JUNIOR POLATKIN
Yeah, he played in the Six-Feet-and-Under, Forty-Years-
and-Older, Indian Spiritual Leader Basketball League.

VICTOR
Kind of a slow league, though, enit? All those old guys
running up and down the court with their drums and
medicine bundles and singing and shit.
(*pounding his leg in rhythm and singing a makeshift powwow song*)
Oh, I took the ball to the hoop and what did I see? Oh, I
took the ball to the hoop and what did I see? General
George Armstrong Custer was a-guarding me! Way, ya, hi,
ye! Way, ya, hi, ye!
(*Junior and Boo join in*)
Oh, I took the ball to the hoop and what did I see? Oh, I
took the ball to the hoop and what did I see. General
George Armstrong Custer was a-guarding me! Way, ya, hi,
ye! Way, ya, hi, ye!

JUNIOR POLATKIN
What about Chief Joseph? He had to be good.

VICTOR
He retired young, man. He will play basketball no more
forever.

BOO
What about Pocahontas? Was she a cheerleader or what?

VICTOR
Shit, old Pokey was a point guard. Strapped on a rawhide
athletic bra to cover up those big ol' Technicolor Disney
boobs and kicked some white boys' asses.

JUNIOR POLATKIN
What about Thomas?

VICTOR
What about him?

ANGLE ON Thomas sitting alone in his chair.

14 ✦ EXT. SUZY SONG'S TRAILER HOUSE—PHOENIX, ARIZONA—DAY

ANGLE ON Suzy Song as she sits alone on her porch.

She is still wearing her business suit, though she holds her jacket in her arms.

She holds it up to her face and breathes in the terrible smell of Arnold's death.

Disgusted, she throws the jacket to the ground.

She stares into the distance.

15 ✦ EXT. OUTDOOR BASKETBALL COURT—DAY

ANGLE ON Victor, Junior, and Boo leaving the outdoor basketball court.

Victor is dribbling the basketball.

Thomas is still sitting on his chair beside the court.

He stands and watches Victor and his pals walk away.

THOMAS

Hey, Victor!

Victor ignores Thomas.

He continues to dribble the basketball.

JUNIOR POLATKIN

Hey, Victor, how come you don't hello Thomas when you know him so easy.

Victor ignores Junior.

Junior and Boo laugh together as if sharing some secret joke.

JUNIOR POLATKIN
(to Victor)
Jeez, look at you, leaving your *se-sen-sab** behind.

VICTOR
He's not my brother!

Junior and Boo laugh harder.

They are having a good time at Victor's expense.

The three continue to walk away from Thomas.

THOMAS
Hey, Victor!

Victor continues to ignore Thomas.

Victor dribbles the basketball.

He fakes left, right, dribbles past an imaginary defender.

ANGLE ON *Thomas standing all alone.*

16 ✦ INT. SUZY'S MOBILE-HOME LIVING ROOM—DAY

ANGLE ON *Suzy Song sitting on her couch.*

She is now wearing a T-shirt and blue jeans.

The room is simple and neat.

A recliner, couch, coffee table, television.

There are many books of all kinds stacked in piles everywhere.

She must be quite a reader.

*little brother

She picks up a beaded wallet, completely beaded with an eagle design, Arnold's wallet.

Suzy opens it and pulls out a photograph.

INSERT SHOT of the photograph of Arnold, Arlene, and Baby Victor.

A happy family photograph.

Suzy looks at the back side of the photograph.

There is nothing.

ANGLE ON Suzy as she picks up the phone and dials a phone number.

17 ✦ INT. JOSEPHS' HOUSE—DAY

ANGLE ON Arlene Joseph.

We HEAR the phone ringing.

She picks it up and holds the phone to her ear.

We SEE the shock, then grief on her face as Suzy gives her the news.

ANGLE ON Victor as he comes through the front door.

Arlene turns to face him.

They share a long look.

Victor is standing very still.

18 ✦ INT. COEUR D'ALENE INDIAN TRADING POST—DAY

ANGLE ON Victor as he stands very still in line at the checkout counter, looking down at a forty-dollar check from his mom.

He looks up to see the CASHIER, a large Indian woman.

VICTOR

Can you cash this? It's from my mom.

The Cashier takes the check, throws it in her register, gives Victor forty dollars.

He looks at the money, knowing it isn't very much.

THOMAS

Hey, Victor.

Victor turns to face Thomas Builds-the-Fire.

THOMAS

I'm sorry about your father.

VICTOR

How'd you hear about it?

THOMAS

I heard it on the wind. I heard it from the birds. I felt it in the sunlight. And your mother was just in here crying.

Victor is suddenly very uncomfortable.

VICTOR

Listen, Thomas. I got to go. I've got things to take care of.

Victor turns to leave again, but Thomas grabs his arm.

THOMAS

Victor, your mom said she only had forty bucks. That ain't enough money to get you to Phoenix.
(*beat*)
I can help, you know?

VICTOR

Help what?

THOMAS

I can help you get to Phoenix. I have some money.
(*pleading, Thomas holds up a glass jar, his piggy bank, filled with paper money and coins*)
I can help.

VICTOR
Listen, Thomas, I can't take your money. Why don't you
go buy a car or something. Go find a woman. Anything.
But leave me alone, okay?

THOMAS
I can get you to Phoenix.

VICTOR
Okay, so you can get me to Phoenix. But what do you get
out of the deal?

THOMAS
You have to take me with you.

VICTOR
(laughing, dismissive)
Sure, Thomas, whatever.

*Thomas watches as the adult Victor walks out the trading post door, which is covered
with red handbills advertising The Last Goodbye Powwow . . .*

MATCH CUT TO:

**19 ✦ EXT. COEUR D'ALENE INDIAN TRADING
POST (JULY 4, 1988)—DAY**

*. . . and then we SEE the YOUNG VICTOR walk out of the trading post into the
parking lot.*

*A few beat-up cars are there, as are a few Indians standing around, laughing and
talking.*

Young Victor is wearing a red T-shirt and blue jeans.

*From behind him, out of the trading post door, the YOUNG THOMAS comes racing
out.*

He is wearing his typical three-piece suit.

He is also holding a burning sparkler firework.

YOUNG THOMAS
Hey, Victor, happy Fourth of July! Look at this. Ain't it cool?

Victor walks over to Thomas.

Together, they both stare at the sparkler.

Thomas is grinning like crazy.

His happiness is infectious.

Victor has to smile too.

YOUNG THOMAS
(cont'd)
Hey, Victor, you want to hold it?

YOUNG VICTOR
Nah, Thomas, it's yours. You hang on to it.

ANGLE ON Young Victor as he is suddenly picked up from behind.

He is scared at first but then we SEE it is Arnold Joseph who has picked up his son.

ARNOLD JOSEPH
Hey, little Thomas, you better get home. Your grandma is looking for you.

Young Thomas smiles and runs away.

Arnold Joseph carries Young Victor over his shoulder to his pickup and deposits him inside.

Young Victor is giggling like crazy.

Arnold gets inside the pickup.

20 ✦ INT. PICKUP (JULY 4, 1988)—DAY

Arnold and Young Victor sit in the pickup.

Arnold reaches into a cooler sitting on the seat between them and pulls out a beer.

He opens it, takes a big drink, hands it to Young Victor.

Young Victor is holding it tightly.

He looks up at his father and smiles.

Arnold smiles at his son.

He shows empty hands and then magically pulls a coin from behind Young Victor's ear.

Arnold starts the car and pulls out of the trading post parking lot, heading for home.

As he drives, he talks.

Arnold is not drunk.

He is just beginning to catch a buzz.

As he talks, Young Victor listens with rapt attention.

ARNOLD JOSEPH

Happy Independence Day, Victor. You feeling
independent? I'm feeling independent. I'm feeling extra
magical today, Victor. Like I could make anything
disappear. Houdini with braids, you know? Wave my hand
and poof! The white people are gone, sent back to where
they belong. Poof! Paris, London, Moscow. Poof! Berlin,
Rome, Athens. Poof! Poof! Poof! Wave my hand and the
reservation is gone. The trading post and the post office,
the tribal school and the pine trees, the dogs and cats, the
drunks and the Catholics, and the drunk Catholics. Poof!
And all the little Indian boys named Victor.

Arnold looks at his son with a big smile, musses his hair.

ARNOLD JOSEPH

I'm magic. I'm magic. I just wave my hand and make it
disappear, send it somewhere else. I can make you
disappear. Where do you want to go, Victor? You want to

go to Disneyland? The moon? The North Pole? I'm so
good, I can make myself disappear. Poof! And I'm gone.

Arnold focuses on the road, dreaming of places he'd go.

He pulls the truck up in front of their house.

Young Victor looks up at him.

> ### ARNOLD JOSEPH
> Here, give me that beer.

Young Victor holds the beer out to his father.

But the beer slips from Young Victor's hand and falls to the seat.

Beer spills.

Angrily, Arnold slaps his son across the face.

> ### ARNOLD JOSEPH
> Look what you did!

Young Victor is crying.

Arnold cleans up the mess, drinks the rest of the beer from the bottle.

He grabs a new beer.

> ### ARNOLD JOSEPH
> Ah, quit your crying. I didn't hit you that hard.
> (beat)
> Now, go see your mom. Tell her I'll be right in.

ANGLE ON Young Victor, still crying, as he climbs out of the pickup.

ARNOLD'S POV ON Young Victor as he runs toward the Josephs' house.

ANGLE ON Arnold as he takes a big drink of beer. He looks out the window.

*ANGLE ON Young Victor as he runs onto the porch, opens the front door, and walks
inside . . .*

MATCH CUT TO:

21 ✦ INT. JOSEPHS' HOUSE (PRESENT DAY)—NIGHT

. . . and we SEE the Adult Victor walk into the house.

He walks through the living room into kitchen.

Arlene Joseph is making fry bread.

She looks up when Victor walks into the room.

> **ARLENE JOSEPH**
> Did you cash the check?

                    VICTOR
Yeah.

                ARLENE JOSEPH
That's all the money I got.

                    VICTOR
I know.

                ARLENE JOSEPH
Is it enough?

                    VICTOR
No.

Arlene drops a piece of fry bread to the floor.

She smiles and rubs her hands.

                ARLENE JOSEPH
Damn arthritis.

                    VICTOR
Hurting bad today, enit?

Arlene shrugs her shoulders.

Victor walks over to his mother, takes her hands in his, and gently rubs them.

22 ✦ INT. BUILDS-THE-FIRES' HOUSE—NIGHT

ANGLE ON Grandma and Thomas standing in their kitchen.

Defying gender expectations, Thomas is making the fry bread.

He kneads the dough and drops it into hot oil.

                    GRANDMA
Do you think Victor is going to take your money?

ANGLE ON Thomas as he shrugs his shoulders.

GRANDMA
I don't trust him, you know. He's mean to you.

THOMAS
He wasn't always mean.

ANGLE ON *the fry bread sizzling in the pan.*

23 ◆ INT. JOSEPHS' HOUSE—NIGHT

ANGLE ON *fry bread sizzling in a different pan.*

WIDE ANGLE ON *Arlene and Victor standing in their kitchen.*

Arlene pulls a piece of hot fry bread from the grease and drops it into a basket.

Victor leans against the refrigerator, drinking a Coke.

VICTOR
Thomas says he'll give me the money. But he wants to go
with me.

Victor reaches over and grabs a piece of fry bread from the basket.

It's hot, so he bounces it from hand to hand to cool it off.

He takes a bite, swallows some Coke to wash it down.

He looks at his mother.

She looks up at him.

ARLENE JOSEPH
You know, people always tell me I make the best fry bread
in the world. Maybe it's true. But I don't make it by myself,
you know? I got the recipe from your grandmother, who
got it from her grandmother. And I listen to people when
they eat my bread, too. Sometimes, they might say,
"Arlene, there's too much flour," or "Arlene, you should
knead the dough a little more." I listen to them. And I
watch that Julia Child all the time.

> (beat)
> She's a pretty good cook, too. But she's got lots of help.

> ### VICTOR
> So, do you think I should go with Thomas?

> ### ARLENE JOSEPH
> That's your decision.
> (beat)
> But if you go, I want you to promise me you'll come back.

> ### VICTOR
> Come on, Mom.

> ### ARLENE JOSEPH
> Promise me.

> ### VICTOR
> Jeez, Mom. You want me to sign something?

> ### ARLENE JOSEPH
> No way. You know how Indians feel about signing papers.

ANGLE ON Arlene as she picks a piece of fry bread from the pan.

CLOSE ANGLE ON on that piece of fry bread being dropped onto a plate.

24 ✦ INT. BUILDS-THE-FIRES' HOUSE—NIGHT

CLOSE ANGLE ON a different piece of fry bread dropping onto a different plate.

WIDE ANGLE ON Grandma and Thomas sitting at the kitchen table, silently eating dinner.

Both look up as they HEAR a knock on the door.

They look at each other and smile.

We HEAR Victor's voice over this.

VICTOR

(V.O.)
Okay, Thomas, I need the money and you can come with
me. But I have a few rules. First of all, you can't wear that
stupid suit.

25 ✦ EXT. RESERVATION ROAD—MORNING

WIDE ANGLE ON Thomas, still wearing his suit, and Victor.

Both are carrying small backpacks.

Victor has clothes and toiletries inside his pack.

Thomas probably has just about everything, but he is definitely carrying his glass jar
piggy bank inside the pack.

Thomas also has a big army surplus canteen hanging from his belt.

They are walking on opposite sides of the road, heading north off the reservation.

We HEAR Victor shouting across the road at Thomas.

They are hitchhiking away from the reservation toward the city of Spokane.

VICTOR
. . . and secondly, I don't want you telling me a million of
your damn stories. And third, we're going right down there
and coming right back.

CLOSE ANGLE ON Thomas, who doesn't say anything.

He just smiles.

We begin to HEAR loud rock music.

26 ✦ EXT. KREZ RADIO STATION—MORNING

As we continue to HEAR loud rock music we SEE a CLOSE ANGLE ON a flimsy
antenna on top of an even flimsier house.

The CAMERA MOVES *down the antenna, follows the wire down the roof of the house, over the eaves, down the wall, to an open window.*

Through the window, we can SEE *the* DISC JOCKEY.

He is an older Indian man in his forties.

He wears mirrored sunglasses and is bobbing his head in time with the music.

He is in his cheap bedroom radio station.

There are compact discs, cassettes, and eight-track tapes all around him.

Various third- and fourth-hand radio equipment surrounds him.

As we HEAR *the end of the song, the Disc Jockey speaks.*

> ### DISC JOCKEY
> Good morning! This is Randy Peone on K-REZ Radio, that's K-R-E-Z Radio, the voice of the Coeur d'Alene Indian Reservation. And Coeur d'Alene people, our reservation is beautiful this morning. It's a good day to be indigenous. It's forty-five degrees in the sun, 8:00 a.m. Indian time in 1998, the year of our Lord, and time for the morning traffic report. Let's go to Lester FallsApart in the KREZ traffic van, broken down near the crossroads. So, Lester, how's the traffic out there this fine morning?

27 ✦ EXT. RESERVATION CROSSROADS—MORNING

ANGLE ON *a white van with* KREZ *clumsily spray-painted in black on its side.*

The van is parked at a desolate crossroads and a figure sits inside the van.

There are no other signs of life.

CLOSE ANGLE *on* LESTER FALLSAPART, *fifty years old, sitting inside the white van.*

He is a short, chubby Indian man with braids.

He is talking into a cellular phone.

LESTER FALLSAPART

A couple cars drove by earlier. Kimmy and James were in the green car. Looked like they were arguing.
(beat)
Ain't no traffic, really.

28 ✦ INT. CHEVY MALIBU—MORNING

We SEE the car radio and HEAR the Disc Jockey's voice over this.

DISC JOCKEY
(V.O.)
There you go, folks! There's no traffic at all. It's 8:02 a.m. Indian time, and it looks like nobody's getting to work on time this morning. As for you school kids, you better eat

your Wheaties in a hurry. First bell rang about fifteen
minutes ago.
(beat)
And I just received a request from Irvin in De Smet. He
wants to hear a sad song. And I told him I refuse to play
sad songs for sad Indians. And that means I haven't played
a sad song in three days. That's a new record, folks. Coeur
d'Alene people, you should be proud of me.

ANGLE ON the Disc Jockey as he starts a new rock song.

29 ✦ INT. CHEVY MALIBU—MORNING

ANGLE ON VELMA and LUCY driving together in a red 1965 Chevrolet Malibu.

They are crazily driving in reverse, so they both look back over their shoulders as they
are driving down the road.

They are good-looking Indian women, although fairly goofy in their mismatched
clothes and weird glasses.

Velma, the passenger, is bobbing her head in time with the rock music.

Lucy, the driver, is stoic, concentrating hard because she is driving the car, full speed,
in reverse.

> VELMA
> Oh, man, I love this song!

> LUCY
> Jeez, you love every song.

> VELMA
> No, but I mean it, I really love this song!

Velma nods her head more vigorously.

She reaches down and turns up the volume on the radio.

Lucy turns it back down.

LUCY
Jeez, I'm thirsty. Get me a beer!

Velma reaches into the cooler at her feet, then stops.

VELMA
Hey, we don't drink no more, remember?

LUCY
That's right, enit? I forgot. Give me a Coke then.

Velma reaches into the cooler, pulls out a Coke, opens it, and hands it to Lucy.

Lucy takes a long drink, her eyes closed in pleasure.

Velma flinches as the car weaves.

VELMA
Hey, be careful! Watch where you're going!

Lucy sets the Coke between her legs.

LUCY
I am watching where I'm going.

Lucy takes off her sunglasses, squints at Velma.

Velma takes off her sunglasses and squints back.

Both laugh wildly.

Then they get all serious.

Then break up laughing again.

Lucy looks toward the road again.

They're still laughing when Lucy sees two people, Victor and Thomas, standing on the road.

LUCY
Who's that?

VELMA

Jeez, it's Thomas and Victor.

Velma and Lucy look at each other with surprise, then both turn around in their seats to look back at the road.

LUCY

What are those two doing together?

VELMA

I don't know.

30 ✦ EXT. RESERVATION ROAD—MORNING

ANGLE ON the Malibu, driving in reverse, as it pulls up between Victor and Thomas, who are still standing on opposite sides of the road.

The rock music fades.

Victor is on the driver's side.

Thomas is on the passenger's side.

Victor is obviously embarrassed to be seen with Thomas.

Thomas is smiling as usual.

31 ✦ INT. MALIBU—MORNING

Victor is on Lucy's side.

Thomas is on Velma's side.

LUCY
(to Victor)
Hey, Victor. Sorry about your dad.
(beat)
You need a ride?

VICTOR

Yeah.

VELMA

(*to Thomas*)
Hey, Thomas, you need a ride?

THOMAS

You bet.

VELMA

What you going to trade for it? We're Indians, remember?
We barter.

THOMAS

A story?

VELMA

(*to Lucy*)
Thomas says he wants to trade a story. What do you think?

LUCY

Sounds good.

VELMA

(*to Thomas*)
Well, then, get your ass in here, Thomas! It's cold out
there.

Velma opens the door and Thomas slides in behind her into the back seat.

THOMAS

(*softly*)
What about Victor?

LUCY

(*to Victor*)
So, Victor, what about it? You want a ride?

VICTOR

Yeah.

LUCY

(*to Victor*)
Wait a second. Thomas is going to give us a story for a
ride. What are you going to give us?

VICTOR
(to Lucy)
I thought Thomas's story was for both of us.

LUCY
(to Victor)
Ain't no story that good. So what will you give us, cousin?

Victor pulls out his wallet, takes out some unidentified amount of money, and hands it to Lucy.

Lucy opens the car door and Victor climbs in behind her.

WIDE ANGLE ON Thomas and Victor in the back seat.

Lucy and Velma turn around to face them.

LUCY
(to Thomas)
So, where's our story? We ain't going nowhere till we get it.

CLOSE ANGLE on Thomas as he closes his eyes.

32 ✦ EXT. PLAZA—DAY

As we HEAR Thomas tell his story in voice-over, we SEE Arnold Joseph standing in a plaza.

He is wearing sixties-type clothes and is holding an M16 rifle as if he were going to club somebody.

THOMAS
(V.O.)
During the sixties, Arnold Joseph was the perfect hippie, since all the hippies were trying to be Indians anyway. But because of that, he was always wondering how anybody would recognize when an Indian was trying to make a social statement. But there's proof, you know? Back during the Vietnam War, he was demonstrating against it, and there was this photographer there. He took a picture of

Arnold that day and it made it onto the wire services and was reprinted in newspapers throughout the country. It even made it to the cover of *Time* magazine. In that photograph, Arnold is dressed in bell-bottoms and a flowered shirt, his hair in braids, with red peace symbols splashed across his face like war paint. He holds a rifle above his head, captured in that moment just before he proceeded to beat the shit out of the National Guard private lying on the ground beneath him. Another demonstrator holds a sign that is just barely visible over Arnold's left shoulder. It reads MAKE LOVE NOT WAR.

33 ✦ INT. CHEVY MALIBU—DAY

CLOSE ANGLE on Thomas as he opens his eyes.

THOMAS'S POV at Velma, Lucy, and Victor, who are all staring at him with their mouths open.

> LUCY
> (to Victor)
> Jeez, did your dad really do that?

> VICTOR
> No way, Thomas is full of shit.

> VELMA
> (to Thomas)
> What happened after that?

> THOMAS
> Arnold got arrested, you know? But he got lucky. At first, they charged him with attempted murder. Then they plea-bargained that down to assault with a deadly weapon. Then they plea-bargained that down to being Indian in the twentieth century. He got two years in Walla Walla.

Lucy and Velma look at each other.

> LUCY
> Well, what do you think?

VELMA

Well, I think it was a fine example of the oral tradition.

Lucy and Velma crack up.

Thomas leans forward to offer them a drink of water from his goofy army canteen.

THOMAS

Anybody thirsty?

34 ✦ EXT. RESERVATION ROAD—DAY

The Malibu, in reverse, drives down the road toward Spokane.

We HEAR the car radio playing rock music loudly.

35 ✦ EXT. ISOLATED BUS STOP—DAY

WIDE ANGLE ON the Malibu, in reverse, pulling up at an isolated intersection with a single hand-painted sign that reads BUS STOP.

The rock music fades as Victor and Thomas climb out of the car.

LUCY
(to Victor and Thomas)
Hey, you guys take care of each other.

VELMA

Yeah, do you guys got your passports?

THOMAS

Passports?

VELMA

Yeah, you're leaving the rez and going into a whole different country, cousin.

THOMAS

But it's the United States.

LUCY

Damn right it is. That's as foreign as it gets. I hope you
two got your vaccinations.

*Laughing wildly, Lucy and Velma pull away, in reverse, leaving Thomas and Victor
alone at the bus stop.*

*ANGLE ON Victor and Thomas, standing beneath the BUS STOP sign, watching
the car pull away.*

36 ✦ EXT. ISOLATED BUS STOP—LATER THAT DAY

*WIDE ANGLE ON the intersection as we SEE the bus pull up close to Thomas and
Victor.*

Thomas is holding his glass jar piggy bank.

*From the BUS DRIVER'S POV we SEE Thomas and Victor standing at the front
door of the bus as it opens.*

Thomas offers up his glass jar of money to pay for the tickets.

VICTOR

Are you sure about this? This is a lot of money.

THOMAS

I'm sure. Are you sure?

VICTOR

Damn right, I'm sure.

Thomas and Victor step onto the bus.

37 ✦ INT. BUS—DAY

ANGLE ON Thomas and Victor standing at the front of the bus, staring down the rows.

Thomas's glass jar piggy bank has been about half drained of money.

THOMAS AND VICTOR'S POV on the TEN PEOPLE aboard the bus, a mixture of odd types: Two old couples that look to be traveling together; a young mother and her young son; two cowboys; a man in a military uniform; a pretty young woman traveling alone.

Everybody is white.

They are all craning their necks, peering out from their seats, to stare at the two long-haired Indians climbing on the bus.

ANGLE ON Thomas and Victor walking down the aisle toward CAMERA.

REVERSE ANGLE ON Thomas and Victor walking down the aisle as all heads swivel to follow their walk toward the back of the bus.

Victor leads Thomas to a pair of seats near the back of the bus.

Victor sits at the window, Thomas on the aisle.

Thomas smiles at the very small white woman, the GYMNAST, blond, mid-thirties, directly across the aisle.

She doesn't smile.

She just looks at Thomas.

She's busy contorting her body into various pretzel-like positions.

Thomas, nodding his head, turns back toward Victor, who is also watching the Gymnast's contortions.

Victor looks at Thomas with a how-the-hell-should-I-know look.

38 ✦ INT. BUS DRIVER'S SEAT—DAY

The Bus Driver settles into his seat and puts the bus into gear.

39 ✦ EXT. BUS STOP—DAY

The bus pulls away from the stop.

40 ✦ INT. THOMAS'S AND VICTOR'S SEATS—DAY

The Gymnast is still twisting her body into strange shapes.

Thomas is staring at her.

He looks back at Victor and smiles.

> **THOMAS**
> *(whispering)*
> I have to ask.

> **VICTOR**
> *(whispering)*
> No, Thomas.

Thomas ignores Victor, turns back to the Gymnast, leans across the aisle, and speaks to her.

> **THOMAS**
> Hey, you're pretty flexible.

The Gymnast looks at him without expression.

THOMAS
Are you a gymnast or something?

GYMNAST
I was an alternate on the 1980 Olympic team.

Thomas turns back to Victor to share the news, but Victor has closed his eyes, embarrassed, pretending to be asleep.

Thomas looks back to the Gymnast.

Thomas smiles.

The Gymnast pulls her leg straight up against her body so that she could kiss her kneecap.

THOMAS
Jeez, I wish I could do that.

Victor opens his eyes and looks at Thomas, disgusted.

The Gymnast looks at Thomas with a slight smile.

GYMNAST
Well, it's easy. Try it.

Thomas grabs at his leg and tries to pull it up into the same position as the Gymnast.

He can't even come close, but the Gymnast laughs.

GYMNAST
Hey, you're Indian, right?

THOMAS
Yeah, my name is Thomas. And this is Victor. We're Coeur d'Alene Indians.

GYMNAST
My name is Cathy. I'm from Mississippi.

Cathy and Thomas smile at each other.

Thomas offers her a drink of water from his goofy army canteen.

THOMAS

You thirsty?

41 ✦ EXT. HIGHWAY—NORTHERN IDAHO PINE
FOREST—AFTERNOON

*The bus rolling down the two-lane highway lined with pine forest on either side. Very
green.*

42 ✦ INT. THOMAS'S AND VICTOR'S
SEATS—AFTERNOON

Thomas is engaged in a discussion with Cathy.

Victor is listening.

CATHY

(bitterly)
I put my whole life into making the Olympics. And then
Jimmy Carter took it away.

THOMAS
Jeez, you gymnasts got a lot in common with Indians then,
enit?

CATHY
Yeah, I guess so.

Victor sits up, leans over Thomas toward Cathy.

VICTOR
Hey, you were an alternate for the team, right?

Cathy looks at Thomas, then to Victor.

She's wondering what Victor is up to.

CATHY
Yeah?

VICTOR

Well, if you were an alternate, then you'd only compete if somebody was hurt or something, right?

CATHY

Yeah?

VICTOR

Was anybody hurt?

CATHY

No.

VICTOR

Then you weren't really on the team, were you? I mean, it didn't matter if there was a boycott or not. You were staying home anyways, right?
(*beat*)
You ain't got nothing to complain about, so why don't you just be quiet?

Cathy is very hurt and angry.

She gets up and walks to the front of the bus looking for another seat.

ANGLE ON Thomas and Victor in their seats.

THOMAS

Why'd you do that, Victor? She was nice.

VICTOR

Nice, my ass. She was a liar.

THOMAS

No, she wasn't.

VICTOR

Yes, she was. Think about it, Thomas. What would a big-shot Olympic gymnast be doing on a bus? Answer me that, Thomas.

THOMAS

I don't know.

                              VICTOR
You know, Thomas, you really need to grow up. Don't you
know anything? People are awful. They'll rob you blind if
you ain't careful. She was probably trying to con you. You
still got your piggy bank?

                              THOMAS
Yeah.

                              VICTOR
Just remember, Thomas. You can't trust anybody.

43 ✦ EXT. HIGHWAY—CENTRAL IDAHO WHEAT
FIELDS—SUNDOWN

Bus rolling down the highway on a two-lane highway.

The setting sun reflects off the green wheat.

44 ✦ INT. THOMAS'S AND VICTOR'S
SEATS—NIGHT

ANGLE ON Thomas and Victor sleeping.

Thomas sleeps with his jacket over him.

Victor sleeps beneath a red blanket.

CLOSE ANGLE on Victor.

He is dreaming, twitching in his sleep.

*The headlights of a passing car illuminate his face and Victor pulls the red blanket
over his face and SWIPES the frame for a:*

                                        CUT TO:

. . . A red blanket fills the FRAME, then is pulled away (which is actually the blanket of a DANCING INDIAN WOMAN who is dancing at a party), and reveals the Young Victor standing in the middle of a big party.

He's very small and lost among all the adult Indians.

Many of the Indians hold brightly burning sparklers and handheld fireworks.

We HEAR loud laughter, drunken conversation, distorted music.

The Indian woman with the red blanket dances by herself.

TWO FAT INDIAN MEN play a rough game of Nerf basketball in the corner, laughing and slamming each other into the walls.

AN INDIAN MAN IN SUNGLASSES, JIM BOYD plays guitar and sings a very sad song, "The Ballad of Arlene and Arnold."

Arnold and Arlene Joseph, both very drunk, are slow dancing together.

Arlene notices her young son.

> **ARLENE JOSEPH**
> Victor, come dance with us.

> **ARNOLD JOSEPH**
> Yeah, Victor, come dance with your old man.

Young Victor joins his parents' drunken dance.

For a few moments, it is a tender, if dysfunctional, family affair.

> **ARNOLD JOSEPH**
> (cont'd)
> Hey, Victor, who's your favorite Indian, huh? Who's your favorite?

> **ARLENE JOSEPH**
> It's your momma, huh? Tell him it's your momma.

YOUNG VICTOR
(softly)
Nobody.

ARNOLD JOSEPH
What did you say, Victor. Speak up, boy. Who's your
favorite Indian?

YOUNG VICTOR
Nobody.

ARNOLD JOSEPH
Nobody, huh? Nobody! Did you say nobody?

ARLENE JOSEPH
He didn't mean it. Come on, tell him, Victor. Tell your
daddy you didn't mean it.

YOUNG VICTOR
Nobody. Nobody. Nobody.

Arnold is hurt.

He kneels down in front of his son and looks him in the eye.

Arnold and Young Victor share a moment of pain and understanding.

Arnold rises to his feet and walks away.

Arlene Joseph picks up her young son and dances a few turns with him.

ARLENE JOSEPH
You got to love somebody, Victor.

She sings along with the sad ballad that plays on and on.

Arnold is shouting and dancing around the party, bumping into people.

*He's angry and celebratory at the same time because he's too drunk to tell the difference
between the two.*

ARNOLD JOSEPH
Nobody! Nobody! Nobody!

Arlene leaves her son to calm down Arnold.

CLOSE ANGLE ON Young Victor as he stands in the middle of the party.

He is a small, lost figure.

46 ✦ INT. JOSEPHS' BEDROOM (JULY 4, 1988)—NIGHT

ANGLE ON Young Victor standing at the foot of his parents' bed.

We can still HEAR the party happening in the living room.

Arlene and Arnold Joseph are passed out on top of the covers.

Beer cans everywhere.

Young Victor climbs up on the bed between them.

He kisses his mother's cheek, then curls up next to his father.

CLOSE ANGLE on Young Victor's face, his eyes closed, his face suddenly illuminated by fireworks bursting outside.

47 ✦ EXT. SILVER TRAILER (PRESENT DAY)—DAWN

WIDE ANGLE ON the sun as it rises.

CAMERA MOVES to Arnold's silver trailer in Phoenix where we SEE Suzy Song, wearing a T-shirt and blue jeans, as she stuffs her very nice business suit into a burning barrel.

CLOSE ANGLE ON the burning barrel.

MATCH CUT TO:

48 ✦ EXT. ROADSIDE DINER—SOUTHERN IDAHO SCABLANDS—MORNING

CLOSE ANGLE ON a burning match.

ANGLE ON the Bus Driver lighting his cigarette, leaning against the bus.

WIDE ANGLE ON the bus, empty, parked outside a diner.

We SEE the passengers inside the diner.

49 ♦ INT. ROADSIDE DINER—MORNING

ANGLE ON Thomas and Victor sharing a table.

Thomas looks over his shoulder toward the door.

ANGLE ON the Gymnast seated near the door, watching it with excitement.

ANGLE ON Thomas and Victor.

> **THOMAS**
> See there, she's waiting for someone.

Victor looks up from his breakfast, grunts, and goes back to eating.

Victor ignores Thomas.

ANGLE ON the door as AN OLD WHITE MAN comes in and the Gymnast rushes to greet him.

They hug and leave the diner.

ANGLE ON Thomas watching them leave, then he turns back to Victor.

They eat in silence for a few moments.

> **THOMAS**
> Must have been her dad, enit?

Victor ignores him.

Thomas pokes at his breakfast.

> **THOMAS**
> You know, your dad took me to Denny's once.

VICTOR
Thomas, I've heard this story a thousand times.

THOMAS
(ignoring Victor)
Yeah, it was the summer he left. You and I were twelve, enit?

Victor continues to ignore Thomas.

THOMAS
Yeah, I had this dream, you know? And the dream told me to go to Spokane, to stand by the Falls, you know those ones by the YMCA?

Victor doesn't respond.

THOMAS
Yeah, so I walked there, you know? I mean, I didn't have no car. I didn't have no license. I was twelve years old! It took me all day, but I walked there, and stood on this bridge over the Falls, waiting for a sign.

CLOSE ANGLE on Thomas as he closes his eyes.

50 ✦ EXT. SPOKANE FALLS (1988, THOMAS'S STORY)—DAY

We HEAR Thomas's voice as we SEE a bridge over Spokane Falls.

We SEE only the twelve-year-old Thomas and Arnold Joseph silently standing side by side on the bridge, staring down at the water.

Young Thomas looks up from the water at Arnold.

Arnold looks down at Young Thomas and puts his arm on his small shoulders.

As this happens, we HEAR adult Thomas speak in voice-over.

THOMAS
(V.O.)
I must have been waiting there for a couple hours. It was

during the World's Fair, remember? All sorts of people walking around. But I just watched the water. It was beautiful. I kept hoping I'd see some salmon, but there ain't any salmon left in the river no more. Then I hear this voice: "Hey, what the hell you doing here?" It was your dad yelling at me. He keeps yelling: "I asked you what the hell you're doing here?" So I told him I was waiting for a vision and he just laughed. He said: "All you're going to get around here is mugged!"

51 ✦ INT. DINER (PRESENT DAY)—MORNING

CLOSE ANGLE ON the adult Thomas opening his eyes.

ANGLE ON Victor and Thomas.

> **THOMAS**
> Then he took me to Denny's. It was afternoon, you know? But I still had the Grand Slam Breakfast. Two eggs, two sausages, two pieces of bacon, and two pancakes. And some orange juice. And some milk. Sometimes, it's a good day to die. Sometimes, it's a good day to have breakfast.

Victor stares at Thomas.

Thomas looks at Victor, looks down at his breakfast, shrugs his shoulders, and takes a bite.

Victor throws his napkin down on his plate.

He stands at the table, walks to the bathroom.

ANGLE ON Thomas as he watches Victor walk away.

52 ✦ INT. DINER'S BATHROOM—MORNING

ANGLE ON Victor's back as he stands at the bathroom mirror.

The entire bathroom is painted stark white except for the doorknob, which is red.

We SEE Victor's face in the mirror, and we can also SEE the door and its red knob behind him in the glass.

CLOSE ANGLE on Victor's reflection in the mirror.

We HEAR the rhythmic sound of glass being broken: SMASH, SMASH, SMASH.

Victor ducks his head out of FRAME.

We SEE an empty mirror and then . . .

MATCH CUT TO:

53 ✦ INT. YELLOW PICKUP (JULY 5, 1988)—
MORNING

From inside the pickup, we SEE out the window into an empty sky.

We continue to HEAR the SMASH, SMASH, SMASH of broken glass.

VERY CLOSE ANGLE ON Young Victor's face as he lifts his head and rises into FRAME.

He is very angry.

He is obviously engaged in some action but we cannot quite see what he is doing.

54 ✦ INT. JOSEPHS' HOUSE (JULY 5, 1988)—
MORNING

In the bedroom, we HEAR the glass SMASH, SMASH, SMASH as Arlene Joseph slowly wakes up.

She wonders about the noise.

She tries to wake up her husband but he doesn't budge.

She gets out of bed and goes to the bedroom window.

Over her shoulder, we SEE Young Victor is smashing full beer bottles against his father's pickup.

Beer and glass explode everywhere.

ANGLE ON Arlene as she reacts to this terrible sight.

We then HEAR her voice.

> ARLENE JOSEPH
> (V.O.)
> We ain't doing this no more! You hear me? No more! We're done with it.

55 ✦ INT. JOSEPHS' HOUSE (JULY 5, 1988)— MORNING

Arlene and Arnold are arguing in the front room.

This is the morning after the Fourth of July party.

There are empty beer cans, used fireworks, and unconscious Indians everywhere.

Young Victor watches his parents argue.

> ARLENE JOSEPH
> It's over! No more drinking! You hear me? No more!

Arnold looks at Arlene, at Young Victor.

He walks toward the front door, ready to leave.

He starts to open it.

Arlene walks over to stop him.

She grabs him from behind.

He turns and backhands her.

She falls to the floor.

Arnold is shocked by what he did.

He looks at his hand.

Then his face hardens.

Arlene stands quickly and confidently.

She stares hard at Arnold, challenging him without words.

56 ✦ EXT. JOSEPHS' PORCH (JULY 5, 1988)— MORNING

The yellow pickup is parked in front of the house.

Arnold slams open the door, comes storming out.

He's wearing a red shirt and blue jeans, black cowboy boots.

He is carrying a suitcase.

Arlene Joseph comes out after him, with an armful of his clothes.

She throws the clothes after him.

ARLENE JOSEPH
If you leave now, don't you ever come back! You hear me,
don't you ever come back!

Arnold doesn't say a word.

He climbs into the yellow pickup and pulls away slowly.

Then Young Victor comes bursting out of the front door, running after his father.

He runs past his mother, jumps off porch, and chases his father's pickup.

Young Victor is screaming and crying.

Young Victor catches up to the pickup and jumps in the open bed.

Arnold stops the pickup, gets out, and grabs Young Victor from the truck bed.

Young Victor grabs onto his father, holding him tightly.

Arnold hugs him back for a moment, then breaks his hold, and sets Young Victor down on the road.

Young Victor is crying.

Arlene comes running up and grabs Young Victor from behind.

Arnold climbs back in the pickup and pulls away.

ANGLE ON Arlene and Young Victor in the rear view mirror of the pickup as it pulls away.

57 ✦ INT. JOSEPHS' HOUSE (JULY 5, 1988)—DAY

ANGLE ON Arlene and Young Victor standing near the living room window.

Victor is staring out the living room window.

He is switching a nearby lamp on and off, on and off, very subtly doing the Morse code for SOS.

> ARLENE JOSEPH
> He's gone, Victor.

Young Victor looks up at his mother.

> ARLENE JOSEPH
> Yeah, your father is magic, enit? A real Houdini, huh? He sawed us into pieces, didn't he? I feel like my head is in the kitchen, my belly's in the bathroom, and my feet are in the bedroom.

Young Victor looks up sharply at his mom.

> ARLENE JOSEPH
> You feel that way, too?

Young Victor nods his head.

OVER ARLENE'S AND YOUNG VICTOR'S SHOULDERS we SEE the Young Thomas Builds-the-Fire standing on the front lawn.

Young Thomas waves at Young Victor, inviting him to come out.

58 ✦ EXT. JOSEPHS' HOUSE (JULY 5, 1988)—DAY

ANGLE ON Young Victor standing on the front porch.

Young Thomas is still on the lawn.

> YOUNG THOMAS
> Hey, Victor, I heard your dad left.

YOUNG VICTOR

What happened?

ANGLE ON Young Victor as he steps off the porch and walks closer to Young Thomas.

YOUNG THOMAS

Why'd he leave?

ANGLE ON Young Victor standing very close to Young Thomas.

YOUNG THOMAS

Does he hate you?

ANGLE ON Young Victor as he suddenly and violently pushes Young Thomas to the ground.

Young Victor jumps on top of the defenseless Young Thomas and begins beating him, throwing punch after punch.

We begin to wonder if Young Victor is ever going to stop when he is suddenly pulled off of Young Thomas by Arlene Joseph.

ANGLE ON *Arlene trying to hold Young Victor, who is kicking and screaming, trying to break loose.*

Finally, he relaxes a bit, allows his mother to comfort him for just a few moments, but then he breaks free and runs away.

ANGLE ON *Arlene kneeling beside Young Thomas on the ground.*

She places his head in her lap.

Young Thomas is bleeding and bruised, but somehow manages a smile.

Then he gets serious.

> **YOUNG THOMAS**
> Why'd Arnold leave?

> **ARLENE JOSEPH**
> Hush, Thomas, hush.

ANGLE ON *Young Victor's face as he is running away, trying to distance himself from his pain.*
He is running faster and faster down the road . . .

MATCH CUT TO:

59 ✦ INT. BUS (PRESENT DAY) — DAY

. . . and we SEE through the bus window as Young Victor is chasing the bus.

As the bus increases in speed, Young Victor falls behind and out of FRAME.

We SEE only the empty road and then CAMERA SLOWLY PULLS BACK to reveal the adult Victor sitting in the bus.

ANGLE ON *Thomas and Victor.*

> **THOMAS**
> Hey, what do you remember about your Dad?

Victor ignores Thomas.

THOMAS

I remember one time we had a fry bread eating contest and he ate fifteen pieces of fry bread. It was cool.

Victor sits up in his seat and looks at Thomas.

VICTOR

You know, Thomas? I don't know what you're talking about half the time. Why is that?

THOMAS

I don't know.

VICTOR

I mean, you just go on and on talking about nothing. Why can't you have a normal conversation? You're always trying to sound like some damn medicine man or something. I mean, how many times have you see *Dances With Wolves?* A hundred, two hundred times?

Embarrassed, Thomas ducks his head.

VICTOR

(cont'd)
Oh, jeez, you have seen it that many times, haven't you? Man. Do you think that shit is real? God. Don't you even know how to be a real Indian?

THOMAS

(whispering)
I guess not.

Victor is disgusted.

VICTOR

Well, shit, no wonder. Jeez, I guess I'll have to teach you then, enit?

Thomas nods eagerly.

VICTOR

First of all, quit grinning like an idiot. Indians ain't supposed to smile like that. Get stoic.

Thomas tries to look serious. He fails.

VICTOR
No, like this.

Victor gets a very cool look on his face, serious, determined, warriorlike.

VICTOR
You got to look mean or people won't respect you. White people will run all over you if you don't look mean. You got to look like a warrior. You got to look like you just got back from killing a buffalo.

THOMAS
But our tribe never hunted buffalo. We were fishermen.

VICTOR
What? You want to look like you just came back from catching a fish? It ain't Dances With Salmon, you know? Man, you think a fisherman is tough? Thomas, you got to look like a warrior.

Thomas gets stoic. He's better this time.

VICTOR
There, that's better. And second, you can't be talking as much as you do. You got to have some mystery. You got to look like you have secrets, you know? Like you're in a secret conversation with the earth or something. You don't talk. You just nod your head.
(beat to nod his head)
See! That makes you look dangerous.

Thomas nods his head.

Victor and Thomas nod back and forth.

VICTOR
And third, you got to know how to use your hair.

THOMAS
My hair?

                              VICTOR
Yeah, I mean, look at your hair, all braided up and stuff.
You've got to free it.

Victor shakes his hair out very vainly.

He runs his hands through it sexily.

                              VICTOR
See what I mean? An Indian man ain't nothing without his
hair. You got to use it.

Thomas slowly fingers his tightly braided hair as Victor talks to him.

                              VICTOR
And last, and most important, you've got to get rid of that
suit, Thomas. You just have to.

Thomas looks down at his three-piece suit.

**60 ✦ EXT. NEVADA DESERT—MORNING INTO
AFTERNOON**

The bus rolling through the desert.

61 ✦ EXT. CONVENIENCE STORE—AFTERNOON

The bus is filled.

The Bus Driver and Victor stand near the bus door.

The Bus Driver looks at his watch, looks at Victor.

Victor shrugs his shoulders.

Victor and the Bus Driver watch the convenience store entrance.

VICTOR'S POV as Thomas comes striding out of the convenience store.

He has taken the braids out of his hair.

It flows in the breeze.

He's discarded the suit.

He's wearing a Fry Bread Power T-shirt and blue jeans.

62 ✦ INT. BUS—AFTERNOON

Thomas and Victor step onto the bus, walk back to their former seats.

TWO WHITE COWBOYS are seated there.

> **VICTOR**
> Hey, those are our seats.

COWBOY #1

You mean, these were your seats.

VICTOR

No, that ain't what I mean at all.

Cowboy #1 stands in his seat.

He's huge.

He looks down at Victor.

COWBOY #1
(quietly and threatening)
Now, you listen up. These are our seats now. And there's
not a damn thing you can down about it. So why don't you
and Super Indian there find yourself someplace else to have
a powwow, okay?

Victor and Cowboy #1 have a stare-down.

Victor loses.

He grabs Thomas by the arm and pulls him to the back of the bus.

*They are looking for another seat but there's only room on the bench seat near the
bathroom.*

Thomas and Victor sit together on the bench seat.

THOMAS

Jeez, Victor, I guess your warrior look doesn't work every
time.

VICTOR

Shut up, Thomas.

THOMAS

Man, the cowboys always win, enit?

VICTOR

The cowboys don't always win.

THOMAS

Yeah, they do. The cowboys *always* win. Look at Tom Mix.
Look at Roy Rogers. Look at Clint Eastwood. And what
about John Wayne? Man, he was about the toughest
cowboy of them all, enit?

VICTOR

You know, in all those movies, you never saw John
Wayne's teeth. Not once. I think there's something wrong
when you don't see a guy's teeth.
(*breaks into song while pounding a powwow rhythm on the seat*)
Oh, John Wayne's teeth, John Wayne's teeth, hey, hey,
hey, hey, ye! Oh, John Wayne's teeth, John Wayne's teeth,
hey, hey, hey, hey, hey, ye! Are they false, are they real?
Are they plastic, are they steel? Hey, hey, hey, hey,
yeeeee!
(*Thomas joins in the song*)
Oh, John Wayne's teeth, John Wayne's teeth, hey, hey,
hey, hey, ye! Oh, John Wayne's teeth, John Wayne's teeth,
hey, hey, hey, hey, hey, ye! Have you seen them? Have
you seen them? Are they false, are they real? Are they
plastic, are they steel? Hey, hey, hey, hey, yeeeee!

THOMAS

Ha, that was a good song.
(*beat*)
Man, those cowboys were tough, though, weren't they?
Tougher than John Wayne, that's for sure.

VICTOR

Thomas, they weren't that tough.

THOMAS

Then how come we're sitting here?

63 ✦ EXT. HIGHWAY—SOUTHERN NEVADA
DESERT—NIGHT

The bus rolling through the dark.

64 ✦ INT. SUZY SONG'S HOUSE—NIGHT

Suzy, in a goofy nightshirt, is kneading dough in her kitchen in the middle of the night.

She's making fry bread.

65 ✦ EXT. SOUTHERN NEVADA DESERT HIGHWAY—DAWN

The bus rolling down the highway into the sunrise.

It's bright and painful to the eyes.

All we can SEE are the sunlight and the shadow of the bus.

66 ✦ EXT. PHOENIX, ARIZONA—DAY

Bus rolling into the city.

Phoenix is a large city, but seems smaller.

No skyscrapers, just low buildings that even look strained in the heat.

67 ✦ EXT. PHOENIX BUS STATION—DAY

Tomas and Victor step off the bus.

They shield their eyes against the bright sun.

Thomas and Victor walk through the bus station, looking confused.

They pass by a drunk homeless Indian man.

Thomas pulls out his glass jar piggy bank, fishes out a dollar bill, and hands it to the Indian.

Thomas and Victor continue walking.

THOMAS
What do we do now?

VICTOR
We walk.

68 ✦ EXT. ISOLATED DIRT ROAD—DAY

ANGLE ON *Thomas and Victor walking down the road side by side.*

As *they walk, the CAMERA MOVES with them.*

THOMAS
How long you think it will take us to get there?

VICTOR
We get there when we get there.

THOMAS
I mean, I just want to know if you have any idea how long
it's going to take. We've been traveling a long time, enit? I
mean, Columbus shows up and we start walking away from
that beach, trying to get away, and then Custer moves into
the neighborhood, driving down all the property values,
and we have to walk some more, then old Harry Truman
drops the bomb and we have to keep on walking
somewhere, except it's all bright now so we can see exactly
where we're going, and then you and I get a beach house
on the moon, but old Neil Armstrong shows up and kicks
us off into space. And then your mom gets that phone call
about your dad being dead, and jeez, he had to be living
in Mars, Arizona, and we ain't got no money, no car, no
horse, so we have to take the bus all the way down here. I
mean, we ain't got nobody can help us at all. No
Superman, no Batman, no Wonder Woman, not even
Charles Bronson, man.
(beat)
Hey, did you ever notice how much your dad looks like
Charles Bronson?

Victor *looks at Thomas.*

Victor thinks of a million cruel ways to get Thomas to shut up, but he resists the temptation.

VICTOR
Thomas, my dad doesn't look anything like Charles Bronson.

THOMAS
Yeah, your dad looks like Charles Bronson. But not the Charlie Bronson of that first *Death Wish* movie.

As Thomas talks, he offers Victor a drink from his canteen.

In frustration, Victor grabs the canteen and tosses it into the desert.

Without hesitation, Thomas leaves FRAME to search for it.

He walks back into FRAME, with canteen, talking as if it had never happened.

THOMAS
(cont'd)
No, your dad is more like *Death Wish V*, the one where Charlie Bronson fights that Asian death gang.

VICTOR

Thomas, will you shut up!

Thomas offers Victor yet another drink.

THOMAS

Thirsty?

VICTOR

Get that thing away from me.

Victor grabs the canteen and throws it into the desert.

Thomas makes to go after it again, but Victor stops him.

VICTOR

(cont'd)
Leave it there, Thomas.

69 ✦ INT. SUZY SONG'S TRAILER—DUSK

From inside, through a window in the very small trailer, we SEE Victor and Thomas walking toward the trailer.

Thomas, without his canteen now, is a little sad.

CAMERA MOVES from window to door, which opens, revealing Thomas and Victor facing someone at the door.

Silence.

REVERSE ANGLE ON Suzy Song standing in the doorway facing Thomas and Victor.

THOMAS

Hey.

SUZY SONG

Hey.

Thomas and Victor are taken aback by Suzy's presence and beauty.

SUZY SONG

One of you must be Victor, enit?

THOMAS

He's Victor. I'm Thomas.

SUZY SONG

I'm Suzy Song.

VICTOR

Is my dad here?

Suzy looks at Victor.

SUZY SONG

Yeah. Hold on.

Suzy disappears into the trailer.

SUZY SONG

(V.O.)
Come in!

CLOSE ANGLE ON *Victor and Thomas.*

They look at each other, then walk into the trailer.

70 ✦ INT. SUZY'S LIVING ROOM

Victor and Thomas stand in Suzy's tiny living room.

They look around.

Suddenly, she appears from around the hallway.

Suzy stands motionless, holding a silver can about the size of a coffee can.

Victor, surprised and confused, looks at the can.

Thomas looks at the can, at Suzy, at Victor, and then the whole circle again.

THOMAS

That's him?

SUZY SONG

Yeah.

Suzy looks to Victor.

SUZY SONG

This is what the undertaker puts them in before you pick out an urn.

Suzy makes as if to give the can of ashes to Victor, who steps back.

Victor will not go anywhere near the can.

He tries to not even look at it.

He will continue to avoid touching it.

Suzy then offers the can to Thomas, who takes it.

Everybody is nervous.

VICTOR

Well, we got to go now. It's a long drive home.

Victor steps toward the door, turning his back to Suzy.

SUZY SONG

But you just got here. I mean, are you sure you guys don't want something to eat or drink?

THOMAS

I'm thirsty. And I'm hungry. I'm both.

71 ✦ INT. SUZY'S HOUSE—NIGHT

CLOSE ANGLE ON a bowl of fry bread sitting on somebody's lap.

CAMERA PULLS AWAY to reveal Thomas, making himself at home, lying on the living room couch with the bowl on his lap.

He also has the can of ashes and his glass jar piggy bank close to him.

Thomas's face is illuminated by the glow of the television set.

We also HEAR generic Indian sounds coming from the set.

> **THOMAS**
> You know, the only thing dumber than Indians on
> television is Indians sitting in front of a television.

*FROM OVER THOMAS'S SHOULDER, we SEE Victor and Suzy sitting at the
kitchen table.*

A big basket of fry bread sits in the middle of the table.

A laptop computer also sits on the table.

An empty red bowl sits in front of Victor.

He is obviously uncomfortable.

> **THOMAS**
> This is pretty good bread, Suzy.

> **SUZY SONG**
> It's okay.

> **THOMAS**
> No, it's good. It's really good, in fact. Hey, Victor, you
> should try some. It's almost as good as your mom's.

> **VICTOR**
> Ain't no bread good as mom's.

> **THOMAS**
> This is pretty close.

*At the kitchen table, Victor grabs a piece of fry bread and takes a bite, expecting it to
be awful, but is surprised.*

Thomas and Suzy watch him with expectation.

                    VICTOR
It's okay.
(beat between bites)
But it ain't even close to mom's.

Victor quietly eats his fry bread.

                    THOMAS
Victor's mom makes the best fry bread in the world.

                  SUZY SONG
Really?

                    THOMAS
Yeah, it's so good they use it for Communion back home.
Arlene Joseph makes some Jesus fry bread, enit? Fry bread
that can walk across water. Fry bread rising from the dead.

                  SUZY SONG
(to Victor)
Is that true?

Victor shrugs his shoulders.

                  SUZY SONG
(to Thomas)
Is that true?

ANGLE ON Thomas as he closes his eyes.

72 ◆ INT. TRIBAL LONGHOUSE (THOMAS'S
STORY)—NIGHT

We HEAR Thomas's voice as we SEE Arlene Joseph standing alone in a kitchen.

                    THOMAS
(V.O.)
Way back when, we were having a feast on our reservation,
you know? A good old feast. We didn't have a whole lot of
food. I mean, we just had a little deer meat, a huge vat of
mashed potatoes, some Coke, and fry bread. But the fry

bread made all the difference. A good piece of fry bread turned any meal into a feast. Everybody sat at the tables and waited for the cooks to come with the fry bread. They waited and waited. Finally, when there was no sign of the bread, my Grandma walked into the kitchen.

As we HEAR Thomas tell this part of the story, the CAMERA MOVES CLOSER to Arlene.

She holds a big bowl of fry bread.

> **THOMAS**
> *(V.O., cont'd)*
> You see, there was a hundred Indians at that feast and there were only fifty pieces of fry bread. Arlene kept trying to figure out what to do. I mean, it was her magical fry bread that everybody wanted. I mean, you know what happens when there are too many Indians and not enough fry bread.
> *(beat)*
> A fry bread riot.
> *(beat)*
> But Arlene knew what to do.

As we HEAR Thomas continue his story, CAMERA CIRCLES Arlene.

> **THOMAS**
> *(V.O., cont'd)*
> You see, Arlene's fry bread was magic. Arlene was magic. She knew how to feed a hundred Indians with fifty pieces of fry bread. She held one piece above her head.

ANGLE ON Arlene holding a piece of fry bread above her head with two hands.

> **THOMAS**
> *(V.O., cont'd)*
> "Listen," Arlene said. "There are one hundred Indians here and only fifty pieces of fry bread."
> *(beat)*
> Everybody was mad. There was going to be a fry bread riot for sure, but then Arlene said, "But I have a way to feed

you all." She took a piece of fry bread, held it over her head, and ripped it in half.

We HEAR loud shouts of protest.

We also SEE Arlene tear the fry bread in half as Thomas finishes his story.

73 ✦ INT. SUZY'S TRAILER—NIGHT

ANGLE ON Thomas as he opens his eyes.

He is still on the couch with the can of ashes and his red bowl of fry bread.

Suzy and Victor are still at the kitchen table.

SUZY SONG
(laughing)
Oh, that's a good story. Is that true?

VICTOR
(breaking into a smile despite himself)
No, it's not true. You're so full of shit, Thomas.

Suzy is smiling.

Victor looks at her.

She is beautiful.

He stares at her as she laughs.

She glances at him while she's laughing.

Her eyes are electric.

Victor cannot take the heat and looks away.

THOMAS
(to Suzy)
So, I told you a story. Now it's your turn.

SUZY SONG
What? You want me to tell the truth? Or do you want lies?

THOMAS
I want both.
(beat)
Tell us how you met Victor's dad anyways.

Suzy stops laughing.

Victor looks at Thomas sharply, then at Suzy.

The mood is instantly serious.

SUZY SONG
(clearing her throat)
Well, jeez. I just moved here a couple years back and as

you can see, there ain't nobody around. Just my place and Arnold's trailer. I saw him puttering around a lot. He was always working on that truck, you know?

Victor reacts to that piece of information.

He knows it's true his father was always tinkering with cars.

74 ✦ EXT. DIRT ROAD (FLASHBACK)—DAY

We HEAR Suzy's voice as we see Suzy walking down a dirt road.

She holds a bag of groceries.

Arnold pulls up in his yellow pickup.

We SEE Suzy lean into the window.

> **SUZY SONG**
> (V.O.)
> I didn't have a car back then. I just walked everywhere or rode the bus. The grocery store's about two miles over that way. So I just walked there. Sometimes, your dad would drive by. At first, he just waved or honked his horn. Then, one time, he stopped and asked if I wanted a ride. He looked safe enough, so I jumped in.

75 ✦ INT. ARNOLD'S PICKUP (FLASHBACK)—DAY

Suzy sits in the passenger seat, Arnold in the driver's seat.

> **SUZY SONG**
> Hey, what tribe are you, old man?

> **ARNOLD JOSEPH**
> Coeur d'Alene. One of the salmon tribes. How about you?

> **SUZY SONG**
> Mohawk.

ARNOLD JOSEPH
Jeez, one of those skyscraper builders, huh?

SUZY SONG
My dad worked on skyscrapers.

ARNOLD JOSEPH
What's your dad do now?

SUZY SONG
Nothing. He's dead.

ARNOLD JOSEPH
What about your mom?

SUZY SONG
She's dead, too.

ARNOLD JOSEPH
Both your parents, huh?
(beat)
So, why'd you come to Phoenix?

SUZY SONG
I was cold.

There is a long silence.

Arnold drops the car into gear, but it coughs, sputters, and dies.

He tries to start it again, but it won't turn over.

He tries again and it still won't turn over.

Arnold is embarrassed.

ARNOLD JOSEPH
Jeez, this hardly ever happens. It starts almost every time.
(beat)
Almost.

SUZY SONG
You want me to say a prayer for it?

ARNOLD JOSEPH
You good at that stuff?

SUZY SONG
I'm the patron saint of reservation pickups.

Arnold smiles.

He tries to start the pickup again.

It sounds even worse than it did before.

ARNOLD JOSEPH
Well, I guess we'll have to walk home.

76 ✦ EXT. DIRT ROAD (FLASHBACK)—DAY

ANGLE ON Arnold and Suzy walking down a dirt road away from the disabled yellow pickup.

Suzy is carrying the bag of groceries.

ARNOLD JOSEPH
You sure you don't want me to carry those? It's a long walk.

SUZY SONG
I think I can make it.

WIDE ANGLE on Suzy and Arnold walking down the dirt road.

We can now SEE that the yellow pickup is broken down within a few hundred feet of Suzy's and Arnold's trailers.

It's not a long walk at all.

CLOSE ANGLE ON Suzy and Arnold.

SUZY SONG
Hey, where you from, old man?

ARNOLD JOSEPH
Plummer, Idaho.

(beat)
You know, I got me an ex-wife and a son up there.

SUZY SONG
So what are you doing down here then?

ARNOLD JOSEPH
I don't know. I guess I'm still trying to figure that out.

Suzy and Arnold walk in silence for a while.

ARNOLD JOSEPH
(cont'd)
Suzy, what's the worst thing you ever did?

SUZY SONG
What do you mean?

ARNOLD JOSEPH

I mean, what's the most evil thing you ever done to
another person?

SUZY SONG

I don't know if I want to answer that.

ARNOLD JOSEPH

Come on. Tell me.

SUZY SONG

Ah, let's see. This one time, at a powwow, I stole some old
Indian woman's purse. She had a couple hundred bucks in
there and I spent it all. Man, that was probably all of her
powwow money, too. I bet she just cried.

ARNOLD JOSEPH

Yeah, that's bad. But there's got to be something worse,
enit?

SUZY SONG

Oh, come on, what about you? It's your turn. What's the
worst thing you ever done?

ARNOLD JOSEPH

No way. It's still your turn. You've got to have done
something worse than steal money.

SUZY SONG

Okay, okay. How about this? Back in college, I slept with
my best friend's boyfriend.

ARNOLD JOSEPH

Oh, now that's bad. You must have broke some hearts that
day, enit?

SUZY SONG

At least three.

ARNOLD JOSEPH

Yeah, just like me. I broke three hearts, too.

We SEE the two are actually very close to their trailers.

It's not a "long walk" at all.

77 ✦ INT. SUZY'S TRAILER (PRESENT DAY)—NIGHT

ANGLE ON Suzy and Victor.

Victor is very uncomfortable.

Suzy continues to tell her story while Victor listens.

> **SUZY SONG**
> Your dad was a good-looking man, you know? And crazy.
> And he was kind of giving me the eye, just a little bit. I
> was thinking, Oh, great, an old Indian guy with cowboy
> boots and a red shirt. Ain't nothing crazier than an Indian
> man in a red shirt and boots . . .

Victor is not ready to have this conversation.

*He stands up from the table and walks into living room where Thomas has fallen asleep
with one arm wrapped tightly around the silver can of ashes and the other wrapped
around his glass jar piggy bank.*

He inspects the living room.

> **VICTOR**
> So, Suzy, do you own this hunk of junk trailer or what?

> **SUZY SONG**
> No, I rent it from this old white guy.

> **VICTOR**
> Is it expensive?

> **SUZY SONG**
> Kind of.

VICTOR

(to Suzy)

Where do you get your money? You got a job or
something?

SUZY SONG

Yeah, I work for Indian Health Service.

(beat)

But I don't know if I have a job anymore. I haven't been
there since I found your dad.

(beat)

I haven't talked to anybody since it happened.

(beat)

Work keeps calling me. The phone keeps ringing, you
know? But I just can't answer it.

Victor digests this information.

VICTOR

Are you a nurse or something?

SUZY SONG

I used to be a nurse. Now, I'm a hospital administrator.

VICTOR

What does that mean?

SUZY SONG

It means I travel too much.

VICTOR

I bet you've been everywhere, enit?

SUZY SONG

I've been to a lot of places since I left home.

Beat.

VICTOR

So, where's home, then?

SUZY SONG

New York.

VICTOR
New York City?

SUZY SONG
Yeah, what's wrong with that?

VICTOR
Jeez, I didn't know there were any Indians in New York
City.

SUZY SONG
There are lots of Indians in New York City. Lots of
Mohawks.

VICTOR
Are you full-blood Mohawk?

SUZY SONG
I'm Mohawk . . .
(beat)
. . . and Chinese.

VICTOR
(surprised)
Chinese? You're kidding!

SUZY SONG
What? You have something against Chinese?

VICTOR
No, no. I just never heard of no Chinese Indians. I mean, I
know black Indians and white Indians and Mexican
Indians, but you're the first Chinese Indian I ever met. Was
it some kind of Bering Strait land bridge thing?

SUZY SONG
No. My mom was Chinese. She was a bartender. She
worked in an Indian tavern in Brooklyn.
(shrugging her shoulders)
That's where my mom and dad met.

A long silence. Victor can't look at her.

                              VICTOR
Did my dad ever talk about me?

Another long silence.

                            SUZY SONG
He said you two were always playing basketball.

Victor smiles.

                            SUZY SONG
He was always talking about some game you and he played
against priests or something.

We begin to HEAR the sounds of a basketball game as we:

                                            DISSOLVE TO:

**78 ✦ EXT. OUTDOOR BASKETBALL
COURT—PHOENIX, ARIZONA—NIGHT**

*STATIONARY ANGLE ON Arnold Joseph standing at the outdoor basketball
court.*

We SEE the dusty court and the hoop.

*He tells the following story to himself, while making fake moves, fake shots, jumping in
place, moving from side to side.*

He seems both drunk and lonely.

                            ARNOLD
            (looking at the ball)
            Everything in the world can fit inside this ball. God and
            the Devil, cowboys and Indians, husbands and wives,
            fathers and sons.
            (beat)
            And how does it all fit? It's about magic, man. It's about
            faith. It's about holding this ball in one hand, and in the

other hand, you're holding the hearts of everybody who's ever loved you.

(*beat*)

You know, this one time, me and my son, Victor, we was playing this two-on-two basketball game against these Jesuits. Man, those Jesuits were in their white collars, in their black robes, and they was pretty damn good. By the way those priests were playing, I coulda sworn they had at least seven of the twelve apostles on their side. I mean, every time I tried to shoot the ball, this storm of locusts would come flying in and blind me. I was shooting in the dark! In the dark, I tell you! But my boy, Victor, he was magical. He couldn't miss. Those Jesuits didn't have a prayer of stopping him fair and square. But Victor, he was only about twelve years old and he was kinda small, so those Jesuits were beating up on him pretty good. They were beating up on him and chanting at him like Victor was possessed or something. And maybe Victor was possessed, by the ghost of Jim Thorpe or something, because he had this look in his eyes that was scary. It was mean. "Come on, Victor," I shouted. "We're playing the Son and the Father here, but these two are going to need the Holy Ghost to stop us!" I mean, the score was tied up and next basket wins, you know? So, the Jesuits had the ball, and this big redheaded Jesuit drove in and knocked my boy over, you know? Just bloodied Victor's nose all up. All that Jesuit could say was "Forgive me." Can you believe that? But my boy, Victor, he was tough. He just wiped that blood on his sleeve, picked up the ball, and took it to the hoop. He flew, man, he flew, right over that Jesuit. Twelve years old and he was like some kind of indigenous angel. Except maybe his wings were made from TV dinner trays! Ha! But my boy, Victor, he was the man that day. He took that shot and he won that game. It was the Indians versus the Christians that day and for at least one day, the Indians won.

Arnold throws the ball OFF-SCREEN as we . . .

MATCH CUT TO:

79 ✦ EXT. SUZY'S TRAILER (PRESENT DAY)—NIGHT

. . . until it comes to a stop at adult Victor's feet.

Victor bends down and picks up the ball.

> **VICTOR**
> So, my dad told you I made that shot?

> **SUZY SONG**
> Yeah.

> **VICTOR**
> Well, I missed that shot. I lost the game.

SUZY SONG

You mean your dad lied to me?

VICTOR

Yeah, and a lie that made me look good.

SUZY SONG

He was a magician, you know?

VICTOR

I know.

Victor walks away from Suzy.

Still holding the basketball, he stands with his back to her.

VICTOR

(very softly)
Did you love him?

SUZY SONG

What?

VICTOR

Did you love him?

SUZY SONG

Yes.
(beat)
He was like . . . like a father, I guess.

This information knocks the breath out of Victor.

He drops the ball to the ground.

VICTOR

A father? He had you fooled, too, enit?

Suzy isn't sure what to say.

SUZY SONG

He quit drinking, you know?

VICTOR

(cynically)
Yeah, he was tricky, wasn't he?

Suzy smiles sadly.

She walks over and picks up the basketball.

> **SUZY SONG**
> Hey, Victor, you ever heard of the Gathering of Nations
> Powwow in New Mexico?
> *(beat)*
> Arnold and I went there to check it out last year. All sorts
> of Indians there. Thousands of them, more Indians than
> I've ever seen in one place. I kept thinking, I wish we'd
> been this organized when Columbus landed.

Victor smiles.

> **SUZY SONG**
> *(cont'd)*
> And your dad and I were sitting up high in the stands. He
> never liked to get too close to anything, you know?

Victor knows this.

SUZY SONG

(cont'd)

And then the powwow emcee called for a ladies' choice
dance. I got to pick my partner, and I picked your dad. "I
don't dance," he said. "I ain't got rhythm," he said. But I
dragged him all the way down to the floor and we danced.
There were mothers and fathers dancing together. There
were brothers and sisters. There were some sweethearts.
And then there was your dad and me.

VICTOR

And what were you two?

SUZY SONG

We kept each other's secrets.

We begin to HEAR a dog barking.

SUZY SONG

(*excited*)
Kafka!

VICTOR

What?

SUZY SONG

It's Kafka, Arnold's dog. He's been gone since I found your
dad.

Suzy runs off in the direction of the barking, toward Arnold Joseph's trailer.

Victor reluctantly follows her.

80 ✦ EXT. ARNOLD'S TRAILER—NIGHT

*Suzy, still holding the basketball, and Victor are walking around Arnold's trailer,
searching for the dog.*

Arnold's yellow pickup is parked in front of the trailer.

SUZY SONG

I'll tell you. That dog is crazy. He thinks he's Indian.

Dogs are Indian.

SUZY SONG

Yeah? Well, he sure loved your dad.
(beat)
Listen.

ANGLE ON Suzy and Victor as we HEAR a dog barking in the distance, then it grows fainter and fainter.

Then it is completely silent.

All we can HEAR is Suzy and Victor breathing.

81 ✦ INT. SUZY SONG'S TRAILER HOUSE—NIGHT

Thomas, unseen by Suzy and Victor, is watching through the window.

Thomas is holding his glass jar piggy bank, nearly empty of money, in one arm and Arnold Joseph's silver can of ashes in the other.

82 ✦ EXT. ARNOLD'S TRAILER—NIGHT

ANGLE ON Victor and Suzy.

Suzy is still holding the basketball and is staring at Arnold's trailer.

Victor, not wanting to even look at the trailer, is staring at Suzy.

SUZY SONG

You know, I'm the one who found him in that trailer. You wouldn't believe the smell. You think it's bad now, you should of been here a week ago.
(beat)
I think I'm going to be an eighty-year-old woman who wakes up in the middle of the night still smelling that trailer.
(beat)

I mean, what makes a person smell like that?

Long beat.

VICTOR
I can smell him.

SUZY SONG
You know, there's a lot of his stuff still in there. Might be something you want to keep.

VICTOR
There's nothing in there for me.

SUZY SONG
Victor, please.

VICTOR
No way.

SUZY SONG
Hey, how about this? If I make a basket, then you have to go inside. Deal?

VICTOR
And if you miss?

SUZY SONG
Then I'll leave you alone.

Victor considers the offer.

He smiles.

VICTOR
Fine. It's a deal.

Suzy takes a few steps toward the basket and takes a jump shot.

She makes it.

Suzy smiles at Victor.

VICTOR

(cont'd)

Nice shot. But I still ain't going in.

SUZY SONG

You know, Victor, I'm not playing some kind of game here.
I'm trying to help.

VICTOR

Trying to help what? I mean, who are you, anyways? You're
telling me all these stories about my dad. And I don't even
know if they're true. Hell, maybe you didn't even know
him.

SUZY SONG

I know more about him than you do.

VICTOR

You don't know anything.

SUZY SONG

I know about that Fourth of July party. The one where the
house burned down.

VICTOR

What about it?

SUZY SONG

I know how it started.

VICTOR

Nobody knows that.

SUZY SONG

Your dad told me how it started. He told me something he
never told anybody else.

We begin to HEAR the same instrumental disco music we heard at beginning of movie.

**83 ✦ EXT. BUILDS-THE-FIRES' HOUSE (JULY 4,
1976)—NIGHT**

Arnold is standing in front of the house.

He takes a long drink from a beer bottle and then throws it into the distance.

He then pulls out a Roman candle firework and a lighter from his back pocket.

He lights the firework and it begins to shoot fireballs into the sky.

He laughs, spins in a circle, and one fireball goes shooting into the open doorway of the house, but Arnold doesn't even notice.

He stumbles around on the yard in front of open doorway and falls down out of FRAME.

We are now looking into a pitch-dark room through an open doorway.

We can SEE only shadows of shadows inside the house.

But then a flicker of flames, just a spark, and then the fire begins to grow.

As the flames grow, CAMERA PULLS AWAY and reveals more and more of house.

Arnold Joseph suddenly RISES into FRAME with his back to the flames.

He is drunkenly oblivious to the burning house.

CAMERA PULLS AWAY as Arnold walks away from the burning house.

CAMERA STOPS as Arnold STOPS.

He turns around and looks at the burning house, then begins backpedaling in terror.

He turns and runs away from the burning house.

CAMERA MOVES with Arnold as he runs away.

But then he stops, turns, and looks at the burning house again.

84 ✦ EXT. DIRT ROAD (JULY 4, 1976)—NIGHT

Arnold's face is illuminated by flames.

He is silent and still for a moment, then he realizes he needs to go back and save everybody, and runs toward the house.

85 ✦ EXT. DIRT ROAD (JULY 4, 1976)—NIGHT

CAMERA FOLLOWS Arnold Joseph as he is running down a dirt road toward the house that is now engulfed by flames.

We also SEE for the first time other INDIANS stumbling around the burning house.

They are coughing, crying, and screaming.

86 ✦ EXT. BURNING HOUSE (JULY 4, 1976)—NIGHT

As at the beginning of movie, Arnold runs up to the front door of the house.

INDIANS are stumbling around outside the house.

They are coughing and gagging from the smoke.

Arnold stops a COUGHING INDIAN MAN.

ARNOLD JOSEPH
Where's Arlene? Where's Arlene? Where's my wife?

The coughing Indian man cannot speak.

He shakes his head and runs away.

ANGLE ON Arnold trying to get in the front door, but the flames and smoke drive him back.

ARLENE JOSEPH is carrying the Baby Victor Joseph, just a few months old, in her arms as she stumbles out of the door.

She had already exited the house.

ARNOLD JOSEPH
Arlene, are you okay? Are you okay?

ARLENE JOSEPH
There are people still in there!

We HEAR a scream coming from inside the house.

There is no way Arnold can make it into the house.

ANGLE ON Arnold Joseph as he runs around the house looking for a way to get inside.

ARNOLD'S POV on a pair of hands hanging outside a second-story window.

The hands hold a baby.

The baby is quiet.

The hands thrust the baby upward into the sky.

The baby is BABY THOMAS BUILDS-THE-FIRE, also just a few months old.

Baby Thomas, wrapped in a blanket, is drifting freely upward toward the night stars, and then falls down out of FRAME until we SEE only the night sky.

MATCH DISSOLVE TO:

87 ✦ EXT. ARNOLD'S TRAILER (PRESENT DAY)—
NIGHT

ANGLE ON the night sky.

CAMERA PANS DOWN to Victor and Suzy.

Neither of them has any idea what to say next.

VICTOR
I don't, I don't . . . I can't . . .
(long beat)
My dad started that fire?

SUZY SONG
It was an accident.

Victor walks away from Suzy.

Then he turns and walks back toward her.

He has no idea what to do with himself.

> **VICTOR**
> He killed Thomas's mom and dad.

> **SUZY SONG**
> He saved Thomas.

> **VICTOR**
> He almost killed all of us.

> **SUZY SONG**
> He saved you.

> **VICTOR**
> My mom saved me.

As if his knees had given out, Victor kneels down to the ground.

He looks up at Suzy with a look of pain and confusion.

He wants to talk but doesn't know what to say.

Suzy kneels down in front of him and takes his face in her hands.

> **SUZY SONG**
> Listen to me, Victor. Your dad talked about that fire every
> day. He cried about it. He always wished he could change
> it. He wished he hadn't run away. But you have to
> remember something, Victor. Your dad ran into that
> burning house looking for you. He did one good thing.
> He came back for you.
> (beat)
> He didn't mean to die here. He wanted to go home,
> Victor. He always wanted to go home.

Victor pulls away from Suzy and stands.

She stands as well.

VICTOR

(firmly)

My dad started that fire.

SUZY SONG

He didn't mean to.

Suzy hugs Victor close.

He holds her tightly.

Then she gently pushes him away, pushes him toward Arnold's trailer.

SUZY SONG

(cont'd)

He's waiting for you, Victor.

88 ✦ INT. ARNOLD'S TRAILER—NIGHT

ANGLE ON the front door as somebody (Victor) rattles the doorknob.

It turns one way, then another, then is furiously rattled.

A sudden thump against the door as Victor throws his shoulder to it, and the door opens.

We SEE Victor stumble into the living room.

The smell of his father's death is horrible.

Victor covers his mouth and nose, sick to his stomach, wanting to leave immediately, but knowing that he must search the house.

The CAMERA FOLLOWS Victor as he walks from room to room, in search of some trace of himself.

We began to HEAR a very familiar sad song, "The Ballad of Arlene and Arnold."

That same sad song keeps playing throughout the scene.

Victor walks into the kitchen and opens the refrigerator and checks the contents.

He pulls out a Tupperware container filled with something.

He shakes it a little and then returns it to the fridge, leaving the door open.

He opens all of the cupboard doors, looks inside, and then leaves the cupboard doors open.

In fact, during this search, throughout the entire trailer, Victor opens every drawer, jar, container, cabinet, and door he can find, and leaves them open after he inspects their contents.

He also rubs his hands along all of the maps hanging on the walls of the trailer.

In the living room, he picks up books and magazines, and drops them to the floor.

In the bathroom, he opens up jars of cologne and shaving cream.

Finally, he comes to the bedroom.

He looks at the bed.

That bed is where his father died.

A red shirt and blue jeans are draped over a chair at a desk near the bed.

Victor sits at the desk.

He looks through the drawers, but finds nothing.

He looks over the top of the desk and finds nothing.

Victor grabs his father's shirt, holds it to his nose, and inhales deeply.

Through all the smell of Arnold's death, Victor is still trying to smell part of his life, too.

Victor digs through the pockets of his father's blue jeans and finds his father's wallet, completely beaded with an eagle design, the same beaded one that Suzy had held earlier in the film when she was calling Arlene Joseph to tell them of Arnold's death.

Victor looks through his father's wallet, and finds no money, but in a compartment behind his father's driver's license, Victor finds the same photograph that Suzy held earlier in the film.

INSERT SHOT of the photograph of Arlene Joseph, Arnold Joseph, and the Baby Victor.

Victor looks at the back of the photograph.

It had been blank when Suzy first held it.

Now, a single word written there: HOME.

ANGLE ON Victor as he stares down at the photograph.

He cannot begin to understand the complex swirl of emotions inside himself.

But he knows he is in mourning for his dead father.

He knows his father kept some small memento of their life together.

Victor has found evidence of himself in his father's house.

Victor is ready to break.

He digs through his father's blue jeans and finds a pocketknife in the other pocket.

Victor stares at the blade for a while, contemplating his options.

Slowly and methodically, Victor begins to cut his long, black, beautiful hair, and drops the strands onto the bed where his father died.

The hair falls like rain onto the sheets.

89 ✦ EXT. SUZY'S TRAILER—NIGHT

ANGLE ON the moon shining brightly.

The yellow pickup is parked in front of Suzy's trailer.

90 ✦ EXT. YELLOW PICKUP—MORNING

ANGLE ON Suzy, Thomas, and Victor standing near the yellow pickup.

Thomas holds his glass jar piggy bank.

Suzy holds the silver can of ashes.

Victor holds the basketball.

Nobody says a word about Victor's raggedly cut hair.

> ### SUZY SONG
> You've got a long road home, enit?

> ### VICTOR
> Yeah, pretty long.

Victor looks at Suzy.

Suzy smiles at him.

> ### THOMAS
> (to Suzy)
> So, what are you going to do now?

Suzy shrugs her shoulders.

> ### SUZY SONG
> Maybe I'll make it to your rez sometime.

Thomas smiles.

> ### SUZY SONG
> Maybe I'll go home. Back to Brooklyn. I've got me some
> cousins there I haven't seen in a long time.

> ### THOMAS
> How long?

> ### SUZY SONG
> (drawing out the vowel sounds)
> A long time.

Suzy looks around.

She pretends to speak to Thomas, but she is actually directing her words at Victor.

> **SUZY SONG**
> Thomas, I figure there's two kinds of people in the world.
> There are saints, the kind of people who live perfect lives.
> Then there's the kind of people who constantly screw up,
> you know? But, every once in a while, they do something
> right. Maybe they only do it right just once.
> *(beat)*
> But one good thing is enough, isn't it?

91 ✦ INT. TRUCK—MORNING

ANGLE ON Suzy standing on the passenger side of the truck.

She is still holding the silver can of ashes.

Suzy leans over and kisses Thomas on the cheek.

He is embarrassed.

She hands him the can of ashes.

Victor, with the basketball at his side, looks at Suzy.

> **SUZY SONG**
> Drive safe, Victor.

ANGLE ON Victor as he smiles and nods his head in agreement.

Suzy leans back from the window.

Victor puts the car into gear and pulls away.

Thomas waves good-bye.

VICTOR'S POV in the rearview mirror of Suzy standing in the middle of the road as the pickup pulls away.

ANGLE ON Victor and Thomas sitting in the pickup.

Thomas is grinning like crazy.

> **VICTOR**
> Jeez, Thomas, your face is going to cramp.

Thomas and Victor laugh.

> **VICTOR**
> Man, make yourself useful. Put some music on.

Still smiling, Thomas reaches down for the radio.

We HEAR rock music.

92 ✦ EXT. ARIZONA LANDSCAPE—NEVADA LANDSCAPE—DAY

The Arizona and Nevada deserts moving by quickly.

We still HEAR the generic rock music.

The light quickly changes from morning to afternoon to night.

The song begins to fade as we pass desert landscape quickly: cactus, sagebrush, sand, low hills, empty riverbeds.

93 ✦ INT. PICKUP—MIDDLE OF NOWHERE, NEVADA—NIGHT

We HEAR radio static. Thomas, with the can of ashes in his lap, is playing with the radio dials.

Victor, with the basketball on the seat beside him, is driving.

> **THOMAS**
> I'm telling you I can find it.

You ain't going to find no music out here. We're a thousand
miles from everywhere. Radio signals don't travel that far.

                    THOMAS
Have some faith, man.

Thomas fiddles with the dials with one hand.

He holds the can of ashes in his lap with the other hand.

We HEAR a faint signal, then lose it, then pick it up.

It grows stronger and stronger and becomes more recognizable.

We hear Jim Boyd's "Father and Farther."

                    THOMAS
           (hopping around in his seat)
I told you I could find it. I told you, I told you.

                    VICTOR
Jeez, I can't believe it. You got some magic fingers,
Thomas.

                    THOMAS
           (looking with wonder at his hand)
Yeah.

94 ✦ EXT. NEVADA DESERT—NIGHT

The moonlight burning over the desert.

We HEAR "Father and Farther."

95 ✦ INT. ARNOLD'S PICKUP IN NEVADA
DESERT—NIGHT

*The radio reception goes bad and "Father and Farther" fades, as we SEE Thomas and
Victor in the truck.*

Thomas still holds the can of ashes between his legs and the basketball is still on the seat next to Victor.

> **THOMAS**
> Victor, do you know how your parents met each other?

> **VICTOR**
> No, not really.

> **THOMAS**
> I know.

> **VICTOR**
> Well, tell me, Cupid. How did my parents meet?

Thomas keeps his eyes open.

As Thomas tells his story, we can HEAR the sounds of the tavern: glasses clinking, laughter, conversation, pool being played, music.

> **THOMAS**
> Well, your dad and your uncle Alphonse were sitting in the Powwow Tavern when your mom comes walking in. Now, your mom was really tall back then and nobody had ever seen her before. So, when she comes walking in all tall and brown and beautiful, your uncle Alphonse leans in close to your dad and says, "She's real tall, enit?" And your dad smiles and he says, "Yeah, real tall." And your uncle Alphonse, he says, "Jeez, what tribe you think she is?" And your dad, he smiles some more and says, "Amazon." And your uncle Alphonse, he was never all that smart, he says, "Ain't their reservation down in Arizona?"

Victor looks at Thomas and smiles.

> **THOMAS**
> Yeah, it's true. And your mom and dad two-stepped all night long to Hank Williams, man.

96 ✦ INT. COEUR D'ALENE RESERVATION TAVERN (CIRCA 1972)—NIGHT

We SEE Arlene and Arnold sitting together at a bar.

They have just met.

The bar is empty and quiet.

"The Ballad of Arlene and Arnold" softly plays on the jukebox behind them.

ARNOLD JOSEPH
So, what did you say your name was?

ARLENE JOSEPH
Arlene.

ARNOLD JOSEPH
So, Arlene, who's your favorite Indian?

ARLENE JOSEPH
I'm my favorite Indian.

ARNOLD JOSEPH
Ha! No, really, who's your favorite?

ARLENE JOSEPH
I don't know. How about Hank Williams?

ARNOLD JOSEPH
Ah, Hank, Hank. He was so lonesome . . .

ARLENE JOSEPH
. . . he could cry.

ARNOLD JOSEPH
Yeah, he just had to be Indian.

ARLENE JOSEPH
And even if he wasn't Indian, he should have been.

ARNOLD JOSEPH
Don't you know it? There are some white people who are
too lonesome to be anything but Indians.

ARLENE JOSEPH

How about you? Are you lonely?

ARNOLD JOSEPH

(with bravado)
Sweetheart, I don't think I'm going to be lonely no more.

97 ✦ INT. YELLOW PICKUP (PRESENT DAY)—NIGHT

Thomas and Victor are sitting in the pickup.

THOMAS

I remember so much about your dad.

VICTOR

Sure you do, Thomas.

THOMAS

I remember when he took me to Denny's for breakfast.
After I ran away to Spokane Falls and he found me there. I
told you all about that, enit?

VICTOR

You've told me that Denny's story a few hundred times,
Thomas. Except, sometimes, it's Taco Bell. Sometimes, it's
KFC. And once, just once, it was Pizza Hut.

Thomas looks up at Victor. A long silence.

THOMAS

Well, anyways, your dad was going on and on about you.
Said you were so good at basketball. But he also said
basketball was the only thing you were ever going to be
good at.

VICTOR

You know, Thomas, I'm really sick of this.

THOMAS

Sick of what?

VICTOR

I'm sick of you telling me all these stories about my father like you know him or something.

THOMAS

I do know him.

VICTOR

That's bullshit. He left us, he left me ten years ago. Ten years ago, Thomas! And we, I, haven't heard from him since. And I don't know him. And you don't know him, either.

THOMAS

I know him.

VICTOR

What do you know about him, Thomas? Did you know he was a drunk? Did you know he left his family? Did you know he beat up my mom? Did you know he beat me up?

As Thomas's and Victor's voices began to raise in volume, Victor starts to drive much faster.

Thomas is standing up to Victor for the first time.

THOMAS

Your dad was more than that. You know he was more than that.

VICTOR

What was he, then? Huh, Thomas? You're the expert. You tell me. What was he?

THOMAS

You know, Victor, you got it wrong, man, Maybe you don't know who you are, huh? You ever think about that?

VICTOR

I don't know what the hell you're talking about.

THOMAS

Yeah, I think you do. You've been moping around the

reservation for ten years. Ten years, Victor! Doing what? Playing basketball all day. Telling jokes. You ain't got no job. You ain't got no money. You ain't got nothing.

VICTOR

And what do you got, you goddamn geek? You ain't got no friends. You ain't got nothing either. What do you do all day long? Huh, Thomas, huh?

THOMAS

I take care of my grandma.

VICTOR

And I take care of my mom.

THOMAS

You make your mom cry.

VICTOR

Shut up, Thomas!

THOMAS

You make your mom cry. You make her cry her eyes out, Victor. I mean, your dad left her, sure. Yeah, he ran away. But you left her, too. And you're worse because you've lived in the same house with her for ten years, but you ain't really lived there. When your dad left, he took part of you with him. And you let him, too. You let him.

VICTOR

Shut up, Thomas! Just shut up. It's all your fault. It's all your fault!

Victor and Thomas are driving way too fast down the road.

They are arguing with each other and barely paying any attention to where they're going.

VICTOR

(cont'd)
You took my dad away, Thomas. You took him! He saved your dumb ass in that fire and he wasn't the same after that.

He didn't care about me no more. He didn't care about me.
He loved you. He always loved you.

THOMAS

Quit feeling sorry for yourself.

VICTOR

I wish he would have let you burn in that fire, Thomas! I
wish he would have let you burn. He would've been my
father, then. He wouldn't have left me. He wouldn't have
left me.

THOMAS

He was always leaving, Victor. He would have you left no
matter what.

Thomas holds the can of ashes in the air toward Victor.

Victor pushes it away.

VICTOR

You're lying. You're lying. You don't know anything. You
don't know anything.

THOMAS

Stop, Victor! Stop, Victor!

VICTOR

Everything burned up, Thomas! Everything burned up!
Everything! Everything! Everything! Everything!

Victor is screaming at Thomas.

The truck is speeding down the highway.

Neither of them notice the rise in the road in front of them.

*They speed over the rise and come upon a white Cadillac turned sideways in the middle
of the road.*

Victor slams on the brakes, turns the wheel to avoid the Cadillac, and glances off of it.

98 ✦ EXT. HIGHWAY—NIGHT

MOVING SHOT slowly follows yellow center lines.

On the road, a suitcase, shirts scattered, a hubcap, papers blowing through FRAME, the basketball, a set of golf clubs, and shiny pieces of glass all over the road.

Arnold's silver can of ashes, battered and bruised, sits in the middle of the road.

We SEE the white Cadillac off the right side of the road on its wheels, but its front end is completely smashed.

Victor's pickup is off the left side of the road and its front end is also smashed.

99 ✦ INT. YELLOW PICKUP—NIGHT

Victor has his head back against the seat in the pickup.

His nose is bloodied.

Thomas is rubbing his head.

> ### THOMAS
> What happened, Victor? Is it real?

> ### VICTOR
> I don't know.

100 ✦ INT. WHITE CADILLAC—NIGHT

BURT and PENNY CICERO are buckled into their car.

Burt is in the driver's seat, Penny in the passenger seat.

They are a white couple in their forties.

They open their eyes.

Burt's forehead is bruised and bleeding from contact with the steering wheel.

Penny's face is bleeding.

PENNY
(*tentatively*)
Ginger? Ginger?

101 ✦ EXT. DESERT—NIGHT

Thomas and Victor have climbed out of their truck and come running up to the white Cadillac.

102 ✦ INT. WHITE CADILLAC—NIGHT

Thomas and Victor arrive at the car.

Victor is at the driver's window, Thomas at the passenger window.

VICTOR
Are you okay? Are you okay?

BURT
What did you do to my car? What did you do?

Burt climbs out of the car and pushes Victor out of the way.

Thomas helps Penny out of her side.

Penny is hysterical.

PENNY
Ginger? Ginger?

Burt is pushing her back into the car.

BURT
Stay in the car! You got to stay in the car!

Thomas grabs Burt.

THOMAS
Are you okay?

Victor goes to car to see if Penny is okay.

She climbs out of the car and into Victor's arms.

> **PENNY**
> Where's Ginger? Ginger?

Burt breaks free from Thomas, tries to push Penny back into the car.

Thomas pulls him away.

> **THOMAS**
> Who's Ginger? Who's Ginger?

Penny is in Victor's arms.

> **PENNY**
> *(to Victor)*
> I'm so sorry. I'm so sorry. Burt was drinking and driving too fast and . . .

Burt pushes Thomas to the ground and grabs Penny.

From his position on the ground, Thomas looks to the side of the road and sees another car.

> **THOMAS**
> There's another car, Victor!

Thomas runs over to another car, a red convertible off the road.

The convertible is very damaged.

ANGLE ON HOLLY as she is leaning over JULIE, who is moaning and groaning on the ground.

Both are white women in their twenties.

Thomas runs up.

> **HOLLY**
> Help her, help Julie. She's hurt, she's hurt.

THOMAS
What happened? What happened?

HOLLY
We were just driving and that other car tried to pass us and
it hit us and I tried to stop but I couldn't and I hit the ditch
and . . . help Julie, can't you see she's hurt? Help her!

ANGLE ON Burt and Penny and Victor all struggling together.

PENNY
Ginger!

VICTOR
Who's Ginger?

BURT
Ginger's the dog!

Burt pulls Penny away from Victor.

ANGLE ON Holly leaning over Julie.

Thomas tries to touch Julie.

HOLLY
Don't touch her! Don't touch her!

Julie sits up, tries to stand, Holly helping her.

Burt comes into frame, yelling.

BURT
Don't let her up! Don't let her up!

Julie faints again, and Thomas and Holly catch her, and ease her down to the ground.

Burt is screaming.

Victor runs up and pushes him.

VICTOR
This is your fault!

Burt pushes him back.

BURT
Get your hands off of me! This is your fault. You hit me.

VICTOR
(pointing at Julie)
You see her, that's your fault!

BURT
It's your fault, it's your fault.

VICTOR
You're drunk!

BURT
How do I know you're not drunk, you damn Indian!

VICTOR
Your wife already told me you were drunk!

BURT
Get out of my face!

Burt and Victor pushing each other, ready to fight.

Penny screaming.

Thomas jumps in between Burt and Victor.

Julie coughs up blood.

Holly screaming.

HOLLY
Help her! Help her!

Everybody focuses their attention on Holly and Julie.

Thomas kneels down close to the couple.

HOLLY

(to Thomas)
You've got to help her. Help her!

THOMAS

Okay, okay!

HOLLY

Help her!

THOMAS

Okay!

Julie is coughing and struggling.

Thomas leans over, takes her hand.

THOMAS

Julie, Julie. Listen to me. Listen to me. Listen to me, okay?
You got to stay awake. You got to stay awake.

Julie closes her eyes.

THOMAS

(cont'd)
No! No!
(to Holly)
What's your name?

HOLLY

Holly.

THOMAS

Talk to her, Holly. Talk to her.

HOLLY

Julie, it's Holly. Stay awake. Please, just stay awake.

BURT

That's a dead girl. You're talking to a dead girl.

PENNY

(to Burt)
Shut up! Just shut up!

THOMAS

Talk to her, Holly! Make her remember something!

HOLLY

What? I don't understand. I don't understand.

THOMAS

Tell her a story. A story.

HOLLY

Julie, do you remember when we went to the river. Do you
remember the river?

CLOSE ANGLE ON *Julie opening her eyes.*

SURREAL CLOSE ANGLE ON *Julie and Holly dancing very intimately together.*

ANGLE ON *Holly holding tightly to Julie at the car wreck.*

Julie looks up at Holly.

Thomas looks up at Victor.

CLOSE ANGLE ON *Victor.*

He has never sacrificed himself for anything.

He has never been a hero.

He makes the decision.

VICTOR

(softly)
I'll go for help.

Nobody hears Victor.

He looks around, wondering if he should change his mind, since nobody heard him.

He speaks again, much louder.

> VICTOR
>
> I'll go for help.

> BURT
>
> What?

> VICTOR
>
> I said, I'll go for help.

> BURT
>
> You're crazy. Nearest town must be twenty miles back there. You ain't going to make it. She ain't going to make it.

> PENNY
>
> Shut up, Bert, just shut up.

Bert and Penny arguing, Holly weeping, Julie coughing.

Commotion.

Thomas stands quietly, looks Victor in the eye.

They share a long moment of understanding.

103 ✦ EXT. DESERT HIGHWAY—NIGHT

Victor at the beginning of his run. He looks strong.

104 ✦ EXT. CAR WRECK—NIGHT

Thomas sitting near Holly, who cradles Julie's head in her lap.

Thomas touches Holly's arm.

105 ✦ EXT. DESERT HIGHWAY—NIGHT

Victor more tired now, his running less confident.

He's sweating and breathing hard.

106 ✦ EXT. CAR WRECK—NIGHT

Penny looking for her dog Ginger, calling out its name.

She finds the body on the road.

She falls to her knees, weeping.

107 ✦ EXT. DESERT HIGHWAY—NIGHT

ANGLE ON Victor running, his footsteps echoing in the night.

He is sweating profusely, exhausted.

He is ready to collapse. But he keeps running.

We FOLLOW Victor for a while.

WIDE ANGLE on Victor running through the desert to reveal how alone he is.

108 ✦ EXT. CAR WRECK—NIGHT

Thomas sitting on the road.

Holly holding Julie's head in her lap.

Burt standing off at a distance.

Penny, weeping, holding on to her dog's dead body.

109 ✦ EXT. DESERT HIGHWAY—NIGHT

ANGLE ON Victor running.

110 ✦ EXT. CAR WRECK—NIGHT

Burt pacing around.

Holly holding Julie in her lap.

Penny weeping inconsolably.

> **BURT**
> He ain't going to do it. He's passed out on the road
> somewhere. He's vulture bait.

Holly is unnerved by Burt's pessimism.

She turns to Thomas.

> **HOLLY**
> Where is he? Where is he?

> **THOMAS**
> Victor can make it, you know? He can make it.

111 ✦ EXT. BUILDS-THE-FIRE FAMILY'S BURNING HOUSE (FLASHBACK)—NIGHT

As at beginning of movie, though there is no crowd this time.

It's just Arnold Joseph running across the grass, his arms outstretched . . .

112 ✦ EXT. DESERT HIGHWAY—NIGHT

. . . Victor running weakly, staggering, his arms and legs out of control.

His breathing ragged. He stumbles and begins to fall . . .

113 ✦ EXT. BURNING HOUSE (FLASHBACK)—NIGHT

. . . Baby Thomas falling through the air.

Arnold diving to make the catch . . .

114 ✦ EXT. DESERT HIGHWAY—NIGHT BECOMING DAWN

. . . Adult Victor falling toward the highway.

He is completely, utterly exhausted.

He has nothing left.

He's been running for hours, looking for help.

He hits hard on the pavement.

He looks up from the pavement . . .

115 ✦ EXT. SPOKANE FALLS BRIDGE (FLASHBACK)—DAWN

. . . and sees Arnold Joseph standing on the bridge over Spokane Falls.

Arnold looks at his son, reaches down with his hand.

Victor reaches up with his hand . . .

116 ✦ EXT. DESERT HIGHWAY—DAWN

. . . and finds himself reaching for a MALE ROAD CONSTRUCTION WORKER.

The worker is wearing an orange vest and holding a bright red stop sign.

117 ✦ INT. HOSPITAL HALLWAY—MORNING

Thomas is pushing Victor down the hallway in a wheelchair.

Both in street clothes and various bandages.

Victor's feet are wrapped.

He'll walk with a limp through the rest of the film.

One of the chair's wheels is wobbly, making it difficult to push it in a straight line.

Thomas almost pushes Victor into a wall.

> **VICTOR**
> Jeez, Thomas, can't you drive this thing?

> **THOMAS**
> Who are you to talk about bad driving? You're the one who got us in a wreck.

> **VICTOR**
> Hey, a wreck is a wreck, man. I got cousins who've been in a dozen car wrecks. Ol' Lester FallsApart has been in a car wreck every year of his life.
> *(beat)*
> You and me, we just had one wreck.

> **THOMAS**
> Victor, I think we were in two wrecks last night.

In silence, Thomas pushes Victor to the door of a hospital room.

118 ✦ INT. HOSPITAL ROOM—MORNING

Julie and Holly in the hospital room.

Julie is asleep in the bed, her head wrapped in some serious bandages.

Holly is sitting in a chair next to the bed, asleep, her head on the sheets.

Thomas and Victor stare at the couple.

Holly then wakes up, looks at Thomas and Victor.

She puts a finger to her lips in a "hush" gesture.

Holly walks over to Thomas and Victor where they quietly converse.

HOLLY

(to Victor)
Well, if it isn't our marathon runner. How you doing?

VICTOR

My feet hurt. How is she?

HOLLY

Julie's going to be all right. She's got a serious concussion
and some broken ribs. She won't be running any marathons
too soon, that's for sure.
(beat)
But how are you guys? I mean, the police were just in here.
That Burt guy says the wreck was your fault.

VICTOR

No way. What did you tell them?

HOLLY

I told them what happened. Burt tried to pass us and he hit
us.

VICTOR

That's what happened, right?

HOLLY

Yeah, but Burt said you were chasing him and that's what
made him drive so crazy.

VICTOR

Chasing him?

HOLLY

Yeah, he says you were tailgating him for about twenty
miles. He said you were trying to kill him.

VICTOR

He's a goddamn liar.

HOLLY

Yeah, that's what I told the police. But I don't think they
believed me.

THOMAS

Well, jeez, we probably should get out of town, enit,
Victor?

VICTOR

Yeah.

HOLLY

Yeah, okay. You guys were heroes, you know. Who are
you, anyways? It's like you're the Lone Ranger and Tonto.

THOMAS

No, it's more like we're Tonto and Tonto.

119 ✦ INT. HOSPITAL HALLWAY—DAY

Thomas is pushing Victor down the hallway.

VICTOR

I don't need this thing. I'm not a cripple.

THOMAS

It's hospital rules.

VICTOR

Yeah, yeah. Whatever. We got to get going, man. We'll go
to jail for sure. Where's the truck?

THOMAS

It got arrested.

VICTOR

And the basketball?

THOMAS

It got arrested.

VICTOR

And Dad?

THOMAS

He got arrested, too.

Thomas pushes Victor up to the hospital door, attempting an escape, but they are intercepted by the POLICE CHIEF.

120 ✦ INT. HOSPITAL WAITING ROOM—DAY

HIGH POV DOWN ON Thomas and Victor standing in a very austere room.

The POLICE CHIEF, a middle-aged handsome white man with a weathered face, is casually sitting on a couch.

A large brown paper bag is sitting at the Chief's feet, as are Thomas's and Victor's backpacks.

> ### POLICE CHIEF
> So, boys, please have a seat.

Thomas immediately sits but Victor remains standing.

The Police Chief gives Victor a curious look.

Thomas remains mute and terrified through most of this scene.

> ### POLICE CHIEF
> (cont'd)
> Well, it looks like you boys have gotten yourselves into some serious trouble. Seems like you've been accused of assault with a deadly weapon.

> ### VICTOR
> What deadly weapon?

> ### POLICE CHIEF
> A yellow pickup.

> ### VICTOR
> That's bullshit.

> ### POLICE CHIEF
> Ah, Victor, isn't it?

> ### VICTOR
> Yes. Victor Joseph.

POLICE CHIEF

Well, Victor, there's no need for that kind of language. And I asked you to take a seat.

VICTOR

I prefer to stand.

POLICE CHIEF

I'd prefer it if you sat.

VICTOR

I suppose you'd prefer it if I sat bare-assed on a blanket. But I'm not going to do that either.

The Police Chief is a calm man, but Victor is pushing his buttons.

POLICE CHIEF

Mr. Joseph, is there any particular reason why you're trying to anger me? It certainly isn't going to help your situation.

VICTOR

And what exactly is my situation?

POLICE CHIEF

You've been accused of some very serious crimes.

VICTOR

We didn't do anything wrong.

POLICE CHIEF

You didn't do anything wrong? Well, we have a three-car accident. And we have one dead dog. Everybody else was bumped and bruised and we've got one girl here in the hospital. The doctors assured me she's going to be okay. But we've still got this complaint filled out by . . . Burt Cicero. It says here that you two were tailgating him for twenty miles. Mr. Cicero said he was afraid for his life. And then Mr. Joseph allegedly assaulted Mr. Cicero shortly after the accident. And he says you were drunk. Is that true?

VICTOR

I don't drink.

POIICE CHIEF
You don't drink?

VICTOR
I've never had a drop of alcohol in my life, Officer. Not
one drop.

The Police Chief digests this information.

He understands that Victor is telling the truth.

POLICE CHIEF
Mr. Joseph, I'm not sure what happened out there in the
desert. But I do know that Mr. Cicero is the mayor of
Junction, Nevada. He's a respected and widely admired
public official. And those two girls, well, let's just say their
relationship was not quite ordinary. And you two, you two,
are . . .

VICTOR
. . . we're Coeur d'Alene Indians.

Thomas stands up proudly beside Victor.

POLICE CHIEF
Ah, yes, Mr. Builds-the-Fire. Do you have anything to say
about all of these charges?

THOMAS
We was framed.

The Chief smiles at Thomas's remark.

*At that moment, a YOUNG WHITE POLICEMAN walks into the room with a file
folder.*

He hands it to the Chief.

As Thomas and Victor nervously wait, the Chief reads through the folder.

POLICE CHIEF
(after a long beat)
Well, you two have been accused of some serious crimes

by an elected official of the State of Nevada. But we have here a police report filled out by . . . a Mrs. Penny Cicero who says that her husband is, to quote, "a complete asshole."

Thomas and Victor duck their heads, trying to hide their smiles.

                    POLICE CHIEF
I suppose Mr. Cicero doesn't have much of a case against you . . . especially in light of his wife's . . . ah . . . rather revealing testimony. But there is one last problem.

The Police Chief reaches down and pulls a basketball from the paper bag at his feet and tosses it to Victor.

                    POLICE CHIEF
(cont'd)
Now, I know that's a basketball, but I'm very, very curious about this particular item.

The Police Chief then reaches down and pulls Arnold Joseph's ash can from the bag.

He holds it in his hands as if it were a strange trophy.

Thomas and Victor look at each other.

Thomas and Victor look back at the Police Chief.

                    POLICE CHIEF
    Yes?

                    VICTOR
    (meekly)
    That's my father.

                    POLICE CHIEF
    Your father?

Victor looks to Thomas for support.

Thomas smiles and nods his head.

Victor straightens his back, looks very proud and warriorlike.

He looks back to the Police Chief.

> **VICTOR**
> Yes, that's my father.

121 ✦ EXT. IMPOUND YARD—DAY

ANGLE ON a police car driven by a DEPUTY.

Thomas and Victor climb out of it.

They stand in front of a sign that reads REDEMPTION IMPOUND YARD.

122 ✦ EXT. IMPOUND YARD—DAY

CLOSE ANGLE ON Arnold's battered pickup.

Thomas and Victor stand in front of it.

Both wear their backpacks over a shoulder.

Thomas is holding the can of ashes.

Victor is holding the basketball.

> **VICTOR**
> I can't believe we got out of that hospital alive.

> **THOMAS**
> Yeah, I guess your warrior look does work sometimes.

Victor smiles.

He looks at the basketball in his hands.

He drop-kicks it deep into the refuse of the impound yard.

> **VICTOR**
> Just think, ten years from now, somebody will come across

that basketball out there and they'll wonder how in the
hell it got there.
(*beat*)
Another one of life's little mysteries, huh?

THOMAS
I suppose.

VICTOR
A hundred years from now, some archaeologist will find
that basketball out there, buried in all that garbage, and
he'll think it used to be some sacred Indian artifact.

THOMAS
Yeah.

VICTOR
Thomas, how come Indians have always been measured by
what they've thrown away and not by what they've kept?

THOMAS
I don't know.

A long silence.

Victor looks at his father's ashes in Thomas's hands.

VICTOR
Hey, let me hold on to Dad.

Thomas hands over the can of ashes.

Victor holds it in his hands for the very first time.

VICTOR
(*cont'd*)
Thomas, I'm sorry I got us into that wreck.
(*beat*)
I mean, I'm sorry about every wreck.

123 ✦ INT. YELLOW PICKUP—DAY

Thomas sits in the passenger seat while Victor sits in the driver's seat.

Thomas digs through his backpack and pulls out his glass jar piggy bank.

> ### THOMAS
> Hey, look, it's okay.

Victor smiles.

He digs through his backpack and pulls out Thomas's goofy army canteen.

> ### VICTOR
> You thirsty?

> ### THOMAS
> Hey, I thought you threw that away.

> ### VICTOR
> Suzy and I found it while you were sleeping.

124 ✦ EXT. ARNOLD'S TRAILER—DAY

CLOSE ANGLE ON Arnold's trailer.

Suzy stands near her car in front of the trailer.

She throws a piece of luggage into the car and then walks back toward the trailer.

She stands at the door with a lighter and a piece of kindling.

She flicks the lighter on and off, on and off studying the flame.

125 ✦ INT. YELLOW PICKUP—DAY

Victor and Thomas sit in the pickup.

Victor is trying to start it up.

The ignition whines and whines, but does not start.

The engine must be damaged by the car wreck.

The interior lights flicker on and off and the radio fades in and out with the same rhythm as Suzy's lighter, but the car will not start.

126 ✦ EXT. ARNOLD'S TRAILER—DAY

Suzy is flicking the lighter on and off, on and off.

127 ✦ INT. YELLOW PICKUP—DAY

Victor is trying to start the pickup.

The lights and radio flicker on and off, on and off.

128 ✦ EXT. ARNOLD'S TRAILER—DAY

Suzy lights the kindling and throws it through the open door into Arnold's trailer.

The flames begin to grow.

129 ✦ INT. YELLOW PICKUP—DAY

Victor starts the car.

It roars to life, as if the fire in Arnold's trailer created enough energy to start his pickup.

Victor and Thomas celebrate.

130 ✦ EXT. ARNOLD'S TRAILER—DAY

Suzy is walking toward her car with Arnold's trailer burning behind her.

She climbs into her car.

131 ✦ INT. SUZY'S CAR—DAY

Suzy is in the driver's seat, Kafka the dog is in the passenger seat.

SUZY SONG
Well, Kafka, where do you want to go?

The dog looks at Suzy with love and devotion, but a total lack of understanding.

SUZY SONG
(cont'd)
Did you say Brooklyn? Good idea, boy, good idea.

Suzy rubs the dog's ears.

She drops the car into drive and pulls away.

132 ✦ INT. ARNOLD'S PICKUP—DAY

Victor and Thomas drive away from the impound yard.

VICTOR
Man, oh, man, I am so happy. I thought we were going to have to ride the bus again.

Thomas and Victor laugh together.

Hey, turn on the radio.

Thomas reaches down and turns on the radio.

We HEAR rock music.

133 ✦ EXT. NEVADA DESERT—DAY

The yellow pickup driving down the road.

Rock music playing on the radio.

134 ✦ EXT. NORTHERN IDAHO—DAY

The yellow pickup rolling down the highway.

We can barely make out the landscape in the dark.

The pickup rolls by a sign that reads WELCOME TO THE COEUR D'ALENE INDIAN RESERVATION, POPULATION: VARIABLE.

135 ✦ INT. PICKUP—DAY

Victor and Thomas are singing together.

Both are drinking Coke.

VICTOR & THOMAS
(*singing*)
Oh, my darling, please remember me, dear, I'm the one
that's thinking of you, don't you know that I'll always love
you, way, ya, hey, ya, wa, ya, hey, ya, hey, yee-ha!

They finish the song.

THOMAS
Yee-ha!

                            VICTOR
        That's a good song.

The pickup rolls down the road.

Victor looks around at the landscape.

                            VICTOR
        It's good to be home.

                            THOMAS
        Yeah.

Long silence.

Victor reaches down and puts his hand on his father's ashes.

                            THOMAS
        Well, at least you got the pickup.

Victor looks at Thomas.

They laugh.

                            VICTOR
        Yeah, Thomas, at least I got the pickup.

The pickup rolls down the road.

Victor and Thomas riding in silence.

They know they are coming to the end of their journey.

Victor scans the landscape as he drives.

Thomas looks straight ahead.

Long silence.

Victor takes a long swig of Coke.

                              VICTOR
        Thomas, I want you to know . . . you're right about a lot
        of things.

Thomas and Victor stare straight ahead, unable to look at each other.

136 ✦ EXT. BUILDS-THE-FIRES' HOUSE—MORNING

The pickup pulls up and stops.

137 ✦ INT. PICKUP—MORNING

Victor and Thomas looking very uncomfortable.

                              VICTOR
        Listen, I just . . . well, I want to thank you for everything
        . . . the money and stuff . . .

                              THOMAS
        It's nothing, really.

                              VICTOR
        Well, I just wanted . . .

                              THOMAS
        It's nothing. I mean, who needs money on the rez anyways.

                              VICTOR
        Yeah, you're probably right.

Long beat.

Victor really wants to leave.

Thomas wants to hold on to the moment.

                              THOMAS
        Listen, I know how it is. I know you ain't going to hang
        around me no more. Your friends would give you too much
        shit.

VICTOR
(*weakly protesting*)
Hey, no. I mean . . .

THOMAS
(*firmly*)
I know how it is. It's okay. I understand. I mean, I know
you've got an image to maintain. I know all about your
warrior stuff. I mean, I'm just this goofy storyteller and
nobody likes me and . . .

VICTOR
(*affectionately*)
Thomas . . . please

Victor reaches over and touches Thomas's shoulder.

The first real physical contact between the two.

Thomas is shocked by the gesture.

Victor reaches down and grabs his father's silver can.

He also reaches down and pulls out his father's pocketknife.

*He opens the silver can with the pocketknife and then looks around for something to
pour the ashes into.*

Thomas is surprised.

He thinks quickly, grabs his now empty glass jar piggy bank, and holds it out.

Victor then carefully pours some ash into the glass jar.

Thomas looks at it with wonder.

THOMAS
Are you sure?

VICTOR
Yeah.

Thomas stares at the glass jar for a while.

He is very happy.

He gives Victor a smile.

Then he thinks about their journey.

He gives Victor a sadder look.

Thomas, holding the glass jar, sits beside Victor.

THOMAS
Victor, I'm going to travel to Spokane Falls one last time
and toss these ashes into the water. And your father will
rise like a salmon.
(beat)
He'll rise.

Victor, very seriously, looks at Thomas.

Then he breaks into quiet laughter.

THOMAS
What? What?

Victor still laughing a little, then more serious.

VICTOR
Well, I was thinking about doing the same thing myself.
But I never thought of my father as a salmon.

Victor and Thomas smile at each other.

VICTOR
I mean, I thought it would be like cleaning out the attic,
you know?
(beat)
Like throwing things away when they have no more use.

Victor and Thomas are both serious now.

Thomas climbs out of the pickup.

138 ✦ EXT. PICKUP—MORNING

Thomas walks away from the pickup.

139 ✦ INT. PICKUP—MORNING

Victor watches Thomas walk away.

Then he puts the pickup into gear and pulls away.

140 ✦ EXT. BUILDS-THE-FIRES' HOUSE—MORNING

Thomas walks toward house.

Pickup pulls away.

Thomas suddenly pauses, remembers something, and rushes back toward the pickup.

> **THOMAS**
> Victor!

The pickup stops.

Thomas running up close to it.

141 ✦ EXT. PICKUP—MORNING

Victor climbs out of the driver's side and walks over close to Thomas.

> **VICTOR**
> What is it, Thomas?

> **THOMAS**
> I just want to ask a favor.

VICTOR

Yeah?

THOMAS

Well, I know things are going to be different now that
we're home.

VICTOR

Thomas, will you stop with that? Things are going to be
better.

THOMAS

Maybe. Maybe not. But just promise me one thing, okay?
When I'm telling a story, will you just, once in a while,
stop and listen to me? You don't have to stop every time.
Just once in a while, okay?

VICTOR

Just once in a while?

THOMAS

Yeah, once in a while.

VICTOR

Okay. Sounds like a plan.

Victor turns to go.

THOMAS

Hey, Victor. Do you know why your dad really left?

Victor thinks about this for a long moment.

He could tell Thomas the truth about the fire, but he doesn't.

VICTOR

He didn't mean to.

Thomas nods his head in agreement.

Victor walks back to his truck and climbs in.

142 ✦ INT. PICKUP—MORNING

ANGLE ON Victor putting the truck into gear again, pulling away.

VICTOR'S POV in the rearview mirror as Thomas walks into the middle of the road.

Pickup gaining speed as Thomas grows smaller in the rearview mirror.

ANGLE ON Victor looking straight ahead.

He is wondering about the future.

He reaches down and turns on the radio.

We HEAR the Disc Jockey.

> **DISC JOCKEY**
> *(V.O.)*
> Good morning! This is Randy Peone on KREZ radio.
> That's K-R-E-Z Radio, the voice of the Coeur d'Alene
> Indian Reservation . . .

143 ✦ EXT. SEEN THROUGH WINDOW KREZ RADIO STATION—MORNING

ANGLE ON the Disc Jockey in his bedroom studio.

> **DISC JOCKEY**
> And I just got a news bulletin here that says Frenchy
> SiJohn won five thousand dollars last night playing Bingo.
> Congratulations, Frenchy. All the used car dealers in
> Spokane are eagerly awaiting your arrival. It's 7:35 a.m.
> Indian time in 1998, the year of our Lord, and time for the
> weather report. For that, we go to Lester FallsApart in the
> KREZ weather van out at the crossroads.

144 ✦ EXT. KREZ VAN—ISOLATED CROSSROADS—MORNING

Lester sitting in the white KREZ van parked at the same crossroads as at the beginning of the movie.

He is looking through a pair of binoculars, then talks into a cellular phone.

LESTER FALLSAPART
It's a little bit chilly. Blue sky, a couple clouds. One looks
like a horse and the other one looks like my cousin.

145 ✦ INT. PICKUP—MORNING

Victor listening to the radio.

We HEAR the Disc Jockey.

DISC JOCKEY
(V.O.)
Well, there you have it, from tribal meteorologist Lester
FallsApart. It's a little bit chilly. You better wear your big
coat if you plan on going to work or school today. And
even if you don't go to work or school, it's a good day to
be indigenous. And just remember, my brothers and sisters,
the world is a circle and nothing stops. Nothing ever
stops.

The Disc Jockey punches a button and we HEAR "The Ballad of Arlene and Arnold."

Victor bobbing his head in time with the song.

He sings along a bit, drives for a little while, then notices something.

He smiles.

146 ✦ EXT. JOSEPH'S HOUSE—MORNING

The pickup pulling up to a stop in front of the house.

Victor climbs out of the pickup holding his father's ashes.

147 ✦ EXT. JOSEPHS' HOUSE PORCH—MORNING

ANGLE ON Arlene Joseph standing on the porch.

She looks at her son.

She is surprised to see that his hair has been cut short, but she is very happy.

Tears of joy.

>   ARLENE JOSEPH
>   Is that your father?

>   VICTOR
>   Yes.

>   ARLENE JOSEPH
>   Then you've brought him back.

>   VICTOR
>   Yeah, I guess I have.

Victor walks up close to his mother and hands the ashes over to her.

"The Ballad of Arlene and Arnold" plays behind them.

>   ARLENE JOSEPH
>   Well, I guess he ain't going anywhere this time.

Arlene and Victor laugh.

CLOSE ANGLE ON *Arlene holding her husband's ashes up in the air.*

She has a long moment alone with her husband's remains.

We can still HEAR "The Ballad of Arlene and Arnold" faintly, then louder as we also HEAR a car approaching.

WIDE ANGLE ON *Victor and Arlene as they turn toward the road and watch Velma and Lucy drive by in reverse in their Malibu.*

They honk the horn.

Victor and Arlene wave.

148 ◆ INT. CHEVY MALIBU—MORNING

Lucy is driving.

She's turned in her seat, looking backward.

Velma is the passenger.

"The Ballad of Arlene and Arnold" is playing loudly on their car radio.

VELMA

Crazy Indians made it back.

LUCY

Yeah, never thought they would.

Velma is dancing and singing along with the song on the radio.

VELMA

Oh, man, I love this song.

LUCY

You love every song.

VELMA

No, but I mean it, I really love this song.

LUCY

Hey, I'm thirsty. Get me a beer.

Velma reaches down toward the cooler at her feet and then remembers.

VELMA

Hey, we quit drinking.

LUCY

Dang, that's right, enit? I forgot. Well, get me a Coke, then.

Lucy hands Velma a Coke.

They drive down the road.

LUCY

Hey, look, there's Thomas.

WIDE ANGLE as the Malibu drives by, in reverse, Lucy and Velma honking and waving at Thomas.

"The Ballad of Arlene and Arnold" is blasting from the car, but it fades as the Malibu drives away, then is not heard at all.

ANGLE ON Thomas standing beside the road, grinning like a maniac.

He still holds the glass jar of ashes.

He waves back.

Then he walks up to the front door of his house.

ANGLE ON Thomas standing outside his house.

He holds the glass jar of ashes.

ANGLE ON Grandma Builds-the-Fire sitting on the porch of the house.

She is happy to see her grandson.

She stands from her chair, walks up to him, and takes him in her arms.

She holds him at arm's length.

GRANDMA

Tell me what happened, Thomas. Tell me what's going to happen.

ANGLE ON GRANDMA AND THOMAS as she hugs him close.

ANGLE OVER GRANDMA'S SHOULDER ON Thomas's face as he smiles and then closes his eyes.

As we SEE the following, we HEAR Thomas's voice over this.

ANGLE ON Victor standing on the bridge over the Falls.

He holds his father's ash can in his hands.

He opens the can and a strong wind blows up.

It blows the ash up and out of the can, back into Victor's face.

His mouth is open wide and he is screaming a silent scream.

Instead of his voice, we HEAR the singing voices of ULALI.

We HEAR them until end.

> **THOMAS**
> (V.O.)
> How do we forgive our fathers? Maybe in a dream. He's in
> your power. You twist his arm. But you're not sure it was
> he that stole your money. You feel calmer and you decide
> to let him go free.

MOVING SHOT of the ash as it blows into Victor's mouth, past his head, falls behind him, off the bridge, and down toward the water.

Just before the ash reaches the water, a salmon rises from the water through the ash and splashes back into the river . . .

> **THOMAS**
> (V.O.)
> Or he's the one, as in a dream of mine, I must pull from
> the water, but I never knew it or wouldn't have done it,
> until I saw the street-theater play so close up I was moved
> to actions I'd never before taken.

MOVING SHOT begins to flow up the river, slowly at first, then following the course of the river, quickly through the city of Spokane, to the outskirts, then to more remote areas, then coming to a fork in the river, one fork a stream that feeds the river . . .

THOMAS
(V.O.)
Do we forgive our fathers for leaving us too often or
forever when we were little? Maybe for scaring us with
unexpected rage or making us nervous because there never
seemed to be any rage there at all?

MOVING SHOT then following that stream upstream for a while, as it grows smaller and smaller, then another fork, one fork which is a small creek, following that creek, which grows smaller and smaller.

As we FOLLOW the creek, more and more Indians start appearing beside the creek . . .

THOMAS
(V.O.)
Do we forgive our fathers for marrying or not marrying
our mothers? For divorcing or not divorcing our mothers?
And shall we forgive them for their excesses of warmth or
coldness?

MOVING SHOT very quickly up the creek now as we see a group of people standing ahead at the very source of the river.

MOVING SHOT toward them quickly, then slowing, and stopping on them . . .

THOMAS
(V.O.)
Shall we forgive them for pushing or leaning? For shutting
doors? For speaking only through layers of cloth, or never
speaking, or never being silent?

ANGLE ON the Young Victor and the Young Thomas standing together.

Behind them, Arlene Joseph, Grandma Builds-the-Fire, Suzy Song, the adult Victor, and the adult Thomas.

THOMAS
(V.O., cont'd)
Do we forgive our fathers in our age or in theirs? Or in

their deaths? Saying it to them or not saying it? If we
forgive our fathers, what is left?

CLOSER ANGLE ON *the Young Thomas and the Young Victor as they suddenly
take each other's hands . . .*

WIDER ANGLE ON *the group, creek in the foreground, as Arnold Joseph rises
suddenly from the water, his back to us.*

He walks toward the shore.

SCENE NOTES

✦ *Prologue:* The voice-over that begins over black was recorded by John Trudell as the Disc Jockey, instead of a female actor, but we found the humor to be an odd contrast with the seriousness and tragedy of the house fire.

Ironically enough, after many test screenings and hours of editing, we decided that the audience really did need "permission to laugh" at the beginning of the film. We needed to let the audience know as soon as possible that this film was going to be funny as well as dramatic. But we still had the problem of juxtaposing any kind of humorous opening with the deadly seriousness of the house fire.

So we decided that we should place the Disc Jockey and Lester FallsApart at the beginning of the film, but we didn't want them to be too funny. We were looking for "kind of funny, but not so funny that we trivialize the house fire." Since we knew that we would use all of the available dialogue of Disc Jockey and Lester later in the film, we had to create new dialogue for them both. And since this new opening would take place twenty-some years before any of the close-up footage we already had of the Disc Jockey and Lester, we had to use extreme long shots so that we could "pretend" that the two Indian men were much younger.

In the editing room, on a Saturday in Seattle, Brian Berdan, the editor, found the scene of a truck passing by Lester FallsApart as he waited at the crossroads, but I couldn't seem to find the right dialogue for Lester. I sat up most of the night trying to write the dialogue. The next morning,

I tried to write the dialogue as I traveled to Portland for a book fair. I couldn't do it. The dialogue I wrote was either too funny or not funny enough. We were pushing up against any number of deadlines as I left Portland and made the drive back to Seattle.

On I-5, on a dangerously rainy night, I stopped at one rest stop pay phone and was told by the producers that I needed to come up with the dialogue within minutes. By the time I reached the next rest stop pay phone, I had come up with the dialogue and dictated it to Brian Berdan as I stood in the rain.

> **DISC JOCKEY**
> Good morning, Coeur d'Alene Indian Reservation. It's a rainy Bicentennial Fourth of July and time for the morning traffic report. For that, let's go out to Lester FallsApart, broken down at the crossroads.

> **LESTER FALLSAPART**
> A big truck just went by.
> (*beat*)
> Now, it's gone.

> **DISC JOCKEY**
> Well, there you go, folks. Looks like another busy morning.
> And I just received a news bulletin that Maddie and John Builds-the-Fire are hosting a Fourth of July party at their house this evening. And remember, folks, it's B.Y.O.F. Bring your own fireworks.

Thus, we were able to tell a joke that wasn't too funny, but funny enough, and we were able to include some expository dialogue that pointed the way toward the house fire.

✦ *Scenes 1–6*: These scenes were not shot quite as written, and we seemed to lose some narrative drive because of it. At the beginning, we had propane tanks shooting flames out the doors and windows. This was our "controlled" fire and we were able to shoot scenes of Arnold running up to the burning house, Arnold trying to get inside the burning house, etc. But when the house was set on fire "for real," the whole place burned down so quickly and so hotly that we simply did not have time to shoot many of the scenes and images we needed.

We certainly had any number of beautiful single shots but there wasn't a consistent story thread running through the shots. As a result, there was a tremendous amount of confusion about what was happening during that fire.

The solution was quite simple. Since Thomas Builds-the-Fire is a storyteller, we needed to have him tell the story of the fire in voice-over. I would love to say that I thought of this solution. I would love to say that the director, producers, and/or editor thought of this solution. I would love to say that anybody directly associated with the film thought of this solution. But, in the true collaborative nature of filmmaking, this particular solution was suggested by Guy Tsutsumoto, the husband of Kathy Kozu, who was ShadowCatcher's office manager at the time.

I wrote many versions of this voice-over during the editing process, writing it to picture as the edit changed. This is the final version:

THOMAS BUILDS-THE-FIRE

(V.O.)
On July 4, 1976, my mother and father celebrated white
people's independence by hosting the largest house party
in Coeur d'Alene tribal history. I mean, every Indian in the
world was there. And then, at three in the morning, after
everyone has passed out on couches, chairs, the floor, a fire
rose up like General George Armstrong Custer and
swallowed up my mother and father.
(beat)
I don't remember that fire. I only have the stories. And in
every one of those stories, I could fly.
(beat)
I was just a baby when Arnold Joseph saved me from that
fire and delivered me into the hands of my grandmother.
(beat)
And Victor Joseph was just a baby too when his father
saved me from that fire.
(beat)
You know, there are some children who aren't really

children at all. They're just pillars of fire that burn
everything they touch.
(*beat*)
And there are some children who are just pillars of ash that
fall apart if you touch them.
(*beat*)
Me and Victor, we were children born of flame and ash.

✦ *Scene* 7: This was shot as written, though we dropped some dialogue in the editing room, and added more of Thomas's voice-over and two shots: one of Arnold Joseph drinking in the yellow pickup and a beautiful overhead shot of Arnold leaving the reservation in his pickup.

THOMAS BUILDS-THE-FIRE

(*V.O.*)
After that fire, Arnold Joseph mourned by cutting his hair,
and he never grew it long again.
(*beat*)
And for years after he cut his hair, Arnold threatened to
vanish, he practiced vanishing, until one day, he jumped
in his yellow pickup and did vanish.

During test screenings, there seemed to be some confusion about why Victor cuts his hair in mourning later in the film. I wanted to make it more clear but I didn't want to spoon-feed the audience. I also didn't want to make haircutting a stereotypical Indian act, done on a mountain-top or something. I mean, the symbolic act of haircutting as mourning exists in all cultures, so this wasn't an issue of generic Indian spirituality. It was an issue of personal spiritual choice. So I came up with the idea of also having Arnold cut his hair in mourning. This draws a distinct parallel between father and son and intensifies their relationship.

During editing, we moved Scenes 26–28 here in order to reestablish the characters of Disc Jockey and Lester FallsApart in the present day and to provide comic relief from the seriousness of the house fire and Arnold's eventual abandonment of his family.

✦ *Scene* 8: This scene was moved to a little later in the film because there seemed to be so many jumps in time at the beginning of the film. We moved from 1976 to 1988 to 1998 in so quick a time that we seemed to lose the audience. As Larry Estes, one of the producers, said, "This movie has three beginnings. Let's try to get it down to two." There was also the annoying problem of having to throw so many title cards on the screen in the effort to explain exactly where and when the action was taking place.

Casting note: When I first saw Cody Lightning and Simon Baker together on-set, I panicked because I thought we had cast them wrong. I thought Cody should play Young Thomas and Simon should play Young Victor. I tried to convince everybody to switch them at the last moment, but I, of course, was completely wrong. This was perfect casting.

✦ *Scenes 9–10*: Before we sold the film to Miramax, we had been attempting to make the character of Suzy more magical and mysterious by injecting more of her into the beginning of the film. We never thought of the opposite. This scene was moved to the middle of the film based on Harvey Weinstein's suggestion that the audience should see Suzy Song's face the first time Victor Joseph and Thomas Builds-the-Fire see her face. It's an incredibly simple editing suggestion that radically changed the tone of the film and of Irene Bedard's performance as Suzy Song. She is now much more mysterious and magical because we see her less.

LESSON LEARNED: When editing, think in opposites.

After Harvey made this suggestion, I sat up all night in a Manhattan hotel room and came up with a revised structure of the first seventeen scenes of the film. I caught a cab to a Kinko's at four in the morning, typed it up, reviewed it with Scott Rosenfelt, a producer, over breakfast, and then by lunch, we were in a Miramax editing room working on a rough edit with Diana Tauder, Miramax's post-production supervisor.

After the rough edit met with approval at Miramax, we took it back to Seattle and Brian Berdan made it all work.

✦ *Scene 11*: I will forever regret that we were not able to shoot this scene as written because of torrential rain on the reservation. Instead, we shot the basketball scene indoors and lost some of the magic. We also lost Thomas's eccentric march toward the court, which would have gone a long way to immediately establishing his character.

On a casting note, all of the actors (and they are all wonderful actors) told us they could play basketball, but they actually weren't all that good. I mean, no actor, no matter how talented, can act like he or she can play basketball well if he or she cannot actually play well. I don't imagine that Robert De Niro has much of a jump-shot. Yes, I know I'm talking trash here but I could probably give our three actors a good game if we played one-on-three. But it really didn't matter in terms of this film. They didn't have to be good at basketball. They just had to love basketball. And they definitely do love basketball.

LESSON LEARNED: When casting for good basketball players, make the actors play basketball during the casting process.

Scene 8, as in the screenplay, was placed here during the edit, establishing a visual and emotional connection between the adult Victor and adult Thomas and their twelve-year-old counterparts.

✦ *Scene 12:* Cut from the film as per Harvey Weinstein's suggestion regarding Suzy Song's first appearance in the film.

✦ *Scene 13:* The dialogue in this scene was substantially cut. It was funny stuff but just seemed to take too long to happen. Also, during my four-in-the-morning Manhattan Kinko's run, I came up with a significant change at the end of this scene. In fact, this change in dialogue completely reversed the theme of the scene. Instead of developing the relationship between Victor and Thomas, this scene now develops the relationship between Victor and his father.

As a result, during looping and editing, we added new dialogue for Thomas and were fortunate enough that a previously unused performance by Adam Beach was emotionally perfect.

> **THOMAS BUILDS-THE-FIRE**
> Hey, Victor, what about your dad?

> **VICTOR JOSEPH**
> What about him?

◆ *Scenes 14–16:* Cut from the film because we wanted to move directly from Victor's question at the end of Scene 13 to the phone ringing in Scene 17.

◆ *Scene 17:* This scene was quite beautiful when played silently, but since we moved Suzy's discovery of Arnold's body to the middle of the film, this scene now needed to be more expository. Hence, we added the telephone conversation between Suzy Song and Arlene Joseph during looping.

ARLENE JOSEPH

Hello?

SUZY

Hello, this is Suzy Song. I'm Arnold Joseph's neighbor down here in Phoenix. I've got bad news. Arnold Joseph passed away.

ARLENE JOSEPH

What happened?

SUZY

He had a heart attack. His trailer is here and his pickup. I think somebody should come get it.
(*beat*)
I'm making arrangements. I'll call again.

ARLENE JOSEPH

Okay. Thank you for phoning.

Brian Berdan found the slow pan across Arnold's trailer and yellow pickup that we use in dissolves during this scene. Believe me, it pays to have a great editor, and Brian Berdan is an all-star editor.

◆ *Scene 18:* Shot as written, though Chris Eyre, the director, and Brian Capener, the director of photography, made the magical flashback transition between Scenes 18 and 19 all the more magical by allowing the adult Thomas and the Young Victor to be on-screen at the same time.

◆ *Scene 24:* This wonderful and eccentric interaction between Thomas and Grandma Builds-the-Fire was inspired. Kudos to the actors, Evan Adams and Monique Mojica, and to Chris Eyre.

✦ *Scene 25:* If you look closely in this scene, in the background, you can see Velma and Lucy driving up in their Malibu. This made story sense as shot, but made no sense as finally edited. I mean, Lucy and Velma don't drive up to Victor and Thomas until a little later in the film. But nobody seems to notice this continuity error.

✦ *Scenes 26–28:* As noted earlier, we moved these three scenes with the Disc Jockey and Lester to earlier in the film, and replaced them with Scenes 143–144, also with the Disc Jockey and Lester. These two guys were extremely popular during test screenings so we wanted to use as much of them as possible.

✦ *Scene 29:* Michelle St. John and Elaine Miles give what may be the most rezziest Indian performances in cinematic history. There is no non-Indian actor in the world who could have given these performances. These performances are not the result of years of training and study on how to "act" like an Indian. They are the result of years of living as an Indian, of years of "being" Indian.

NOTE TO ALL OTHER FILMMAKERS: Cast Indians as Indians, because you'll get better performances.

✦ *Scenes 30–34:* The blocking in all of these scenes is different than written. First, because it was cheaper to do it in fewer shots, to avoid the difficult coverage that would have been necessary if all four characters had been inside the car at the same time, and second, to take advantage of the beautiful landscape and endless blue sky of the Coeur d'Alene Indian Reservation. We were very conscious of photographing the reservation in beautiful ways. Especially since Brian Capener had so much experience with landscape film photography. Contemporary films about Indians always highlight the poverty, the ugliness of reservations. We wanted to show, exactly, the beauty of this reservation.

✦ *Scene 32:* We didn't have time to shoot the scene of Arnold Joseph protesting the Vietnam War. It would have been great to have it, especially since all of Thomas's other stories are visualized on-screen.

✦ *Scene 40:* During editing, we got rid of almost all references to Thomas's goofy army water canteen. It wasn't very funny and it was just one MacGuffin too many. This is an example of overwriting the screenplay.

✦ *Scene 41:* Victor seemed like too much of an asshole to the Gymnast so we wanted to give him a little more reason for being so. During editing, Roger Baerwolf, the associate producer, came up with the Gymnast's monologue and we added it during looping.

CATHY THE GYMNAST
I mean, I was every bit as good as Mary Lou.
I tried out for the Olympics in 1984 but Mary Lou
beat me that time. I had grown, you know? Oh,
those little people, they get all the attention.

✦ *Scene 42:* Cynthia Geary came up with this shot of the Gymnast bent over double as she's talking to Victor and Thomas. Cynthia is a very funny person and a dang good actor. She was amazing during looping, changing the whole performance with different inflections, readings, etc.

✦ *Scenes 44–45:* Chris and I struggled over the magical flashback transition between these two scenes. He wanted to cut it because he felt Scene 45 played too long and wanted to enter into it sooner. I felt the magical transition was too valuable to lose, no matter that the scene may play a bit long. In the end, we kept the magical transition as written.

✦ *Scene 46:* Cut from the film. It was a beautiful, tender scene that simply did not have a logical place in the final edit. But we did use the beginning of this scene as a magical flashback transition after Scene 51.

✦ *Scene 47:* Cut from the film per Harvey's suggestion about Suzy.

✦ *Scene 48:* Cut from the film because Brian Berdan created a magical transition swipe between Scenes 45 and 49 that required us to cut directly to Victor's face.

✦ *Scene 49:* Because of scheduling difficulties, Cynthia Geary couldn't shoot the beginning of this scene. We used a double, but it simply lost emotional impact because we couldn't see the Gymnast's face as she reunited with her father. So we cut it from the film.

✦ *Scene 51:* Because Chris chose not to shoot the magical flashback transition between Scenes 52 and 53, I wanted to create something magical here. In watching the dailies, I saw the two-shoot of Victor walking away from the table and noticed his right arm swing through the frame as he walked. By cutting from this arm swing to a shot of Young Victor walking into the frame from Scene 46, and because the adult Victor and his younger counterpart were wearing similar clothes, we were able to create a magical flashback transition here.

LESSON LEARNED: Let the screenwriter watch the dailies.

✦ *Scene 52:* We used this shot of Victor in the mirror but the doorknob is not painted red. In writing the screenplay, I used red as a memory color, as the image which would trigger flashbacks.

✦ *Scene 53:* Chris chose to shoot this scene from inside the house. I miss the close angles on Victor's face. I would have liked to see his pain.

✦ *Scene 55:* Gary Farmer and Tantoo Cardinal improvised the dialogue and action in this scene.

ARNOLD JOSEPH

(grabbing Arlene's purse)
I told you, all I want is the money I got coming to me.

ARLENE JOSEPH

(grabbing her purse)
Did you hear me? No more drinking, no more.

ARNOLD JOSEPH

(slapping Arlene to the floor)
Let go!

ARLENE JOSEPH

(getting quickly to her feet)
Come on, hit me again!

This is a powerful scene made more powerful by Tantoo's and Gary's performances. When Arlene Joseph stands up to Arnold, she is being the kind of powerful Indian woman I've known all my life.

A SECOND REMINDER TO ALL FILMMAKERS: Cast Indians as Indians, because you'll get better performances.

✦ *Scene 56:* Chris Eyre always wanted to include a scene of Young Victor jumping into the bed of the pickup in the effort to stop his father from leaving. I opposed it, based on safety reasons, but I wrote it into the screenplay and Chris shot it with powerful results.

✦ *Scene 59:* This is, without a doubt, my favorite scene in the film. I wrote it quickly, in one or two drafts, and played it out at my kitchen table with my friend Arthur Tulee, a Yakama Indian. It was funny then and is even more funny now.

✦ *Scene 60:* Cut from the film because it ruined the timing of the joke that follows.

✦ *Scene 61:* When I saw the dailies of this scene, I knew that Chris had shot it incorrectly. The scene was simply not funny enough. So I storyboarded the scene and then told the producers how it should be shot. They reshot the next day. This scene now receives the biggest laughs in the film.

LESSON LEARNED: Let the screenwriter work in the editing room.

✦ *Scene 62:* I was very mad at Chris for undercutting the seriousness of this confrontation by making the cowboys switch hats at the last moment. So, the big cowboy is wearing a goofy baseball cap that's too small for him while the small cowboy is wearing a Stetson that's too big for him.

We probably spent more time editing this scene than any other, trying to create tension with various cuts. Brian Berdan saved this scene.

A NOTE ABOUT MUSIC: I always wanted to include Ulali's version of "Gary Owen," a traditional folk song, in this scene. "Gary Owen" was George Armstrong Custer's favorite song. He had it playing when he attacked Indian camps. So, I thought its use during this scene would be very ironic. I also thought it was one of my brilliant, original ideas, but a few months later, I saw Peter Bratt's film *Follow Me Home* for the second time and realized that he had used "Gary Owen" in the same context. I told Peter I had unintentionally ripped him off, or "paid homage to his film," but he just smiled and said, "Well, that's okay. I ripped it off from *Little Big Man*."

✦ *Scene 63:* During editing, we knew that the film was missing a kind of magic. So I suggested that a real traditional drum group write and record a more polished version of the song "John Wayne's Teeth."

I enlisted my friends the EagleBear Singers to do the work and they came up with a version of "John Wayne's Teeth" that is both beautiful and hilarious.

✦ *Scene 64:* Cut from the film.

✦ *Scene 66:* We never shot this because we were never in Arizona. We shot all of the Arizona locations in the deserts of central Washington State. Pretty amazing, huh?

✦ *Scene 68:* Because Evan Adams improvised and turned a few cart-wheels down the highway, I was able to write new dialogue for him that we added during looping.

> **THOMAS BUILDS-THE-FIRE**
> (*while cartwheeling*)
> Hey, Victor, did you know I was an alternate on the 1980
> Olympic team?

During preproduction, Chris Eyre suggested that Victor throw the water canteen off-screen and force Thomas to trot off-screen, only to come back on-screen with a humorous vengeance. I wrote it in because it was a damn good idea. Chris scored on this one.

✦ *Scene 70:* Irene Bedard improvised a line of dialogue in this scene. It's a very Indian moment.

> **SUZY SONG**
> (*while holding the can of ashes*)
> This is Arnold. He ain't looking so good.

THIRD REMINDER TO FILMMAKERS: Cast Indians as Indians, because they'll give better performances.

◆ *Scene 71:* I wish I could tell you that I wrote Thomas Builds-the-Fire's first line of dialogue in this scene, but Evan Adams improvised it a few months previously while shooting a short film based on the second act of this screenplay.

◆ *Scene 74:* Cut from the film.

◆ *Scene 75:* The first half of this scene was cut from the film, and for me, it is the most painful cut. We had to cut it for pacing reasons and because of performance. When Suzy Song responds to Arnold's question about why she came to Phoenix, I always felt that her response is her most important moment in the film. She was supposed to say "I was cold" with all the pain, loneliness, and mystery in her heart. But Chris felt that reading was too "on the nose" and directed Irene to do a more flippant take of the line. It wasn't a bad reading on Irene's part, it was simply the wrong reading. Irene Bedard is an incredible actor. We chose her to play Suzy because she read that particular line so well during casting. I will miss it forever. As a result, we not only lost a beautiful moment for Suzy Song, we also lost any mention of what tribe she belongs to. Believe me, Indian critics, especially Indian women critics, will notice that Suzy doesn't seem to have a tribe. I mean, we wanted her to be mysterious, but not that mysterious.

LESSON LEARNED: Give yourself performance options in the editing room.

◆ *Scene 76:* I had written this scene so we see that Suzy and Arnold were mere feet away from their trailers. I wanted it to be clear that he had offered to give Suzy a ride, not because she had a long walk ahead of her, but because he was a lonely man. But Chris chose not to shoot it this way. It's a valid choice. As is, the scene is tender and touching. As written, it would have also been funny.

◆ *Scene 77:* We cut a lot of expository dialogue in this scene in order to speed the pace. We wanted to get some idea of who Suzy is, but we also wanted to make sure we kept the story moving forward.

◆ *Scene 78:* As noted earlier, we had to shoot all of the basketball scenes indoors because of weather conditions. Thus, the Jesuit basketball scene was very boring. I had wanted the basketball in the movie to look like *Hoosiers*, but it looked more like an Afterschool Special.

I knew the movie needed more magic and I kept trying to think of ways to create it.

I had visited the set, had seen the basketball hoop outside of Arnold's trailer, had seen the barren and beautiful landscape, and with all that in mind, I conceived of and wrote this scene in one draft, in ten minutes, because Gary Farmer was leaving and I needed to write something great to keep him for another day beyond his original commitment to the film.

✦ *Scene 79:* There's a moment during this scene that points out how great movie moments can be completely accidental.

When Suzy tells Victor that Arnold was like a father to her, he drops the basketball into the dirt. The dust that rises appears to be a ghost floating across the screen.

We cut from this scene to Scenes 9–10, inserted from the beginning of the film, as Suzy discovers Arnold's body. Thus, the second act of this film really belongs to Suzy Song.

✦ *Scene 80:* Cut from the film.

✦ *Scene 81:* Cut from the film.

✦ *Scene 82:* During preproduction, Chris wanted to move the house fire that opens the film and insert it here. I hated the idea. I had always intended the film to open with fire and end with water. It was an elemental decision. But I agreed with Chris that the second act needed more drama. Hence, during a preproduction meeting, I came up with the idea that Arnold Joseph accidentally started the house fire that killed Thomas's mother and father. I felt it was very dramatic and went a long way toward explaining why Arnold left his family.

✦ *Scenes 83–86:* Brian Berdan did an amazing job of intercutting between Suzy and Victor in present day Phoenix and the Fourth of July house fire in 1976. All of this belongs to him.

◆ *Scene* 87: During filming, Adam Beach refused to kneel down to the ground as indicated in the screenplay. Chris and I were both very unhappy with Adam, but in the end, his decision was absolutely correct. There was no way that Victor Joseph would have kneeled at that moment, and Adam Beach knew that better than any of us.

◆ *Scene* 88: Our composer, BC Smith, really distinguished himself with the music here, a combination of traditional Indian sounds, contemporary score, and mutated animal calls.

◆ *Scene* 89: Because we cut Scenes 90–96, and used various landscape shots instead, I wrote a Thomas voice-over which would carry the narrative thread and add a little more poetry to the proceedings.

THOMAS BUILDS-THE-FIRE

(V.O.)
After Victor butchered his hair, he thought the ceremony
was over, so he tore me from sleep at sunrise and we left
Phoenix without telling Suzy good-bye. I thought we were
leaving in a bad way, but Victor didn't seem to care a bit.
He just drove all day and didn't say a word to me, even
though I told him a thousand stories about Suzy and
drought, about his mother and hunger, about his father
and magic. And then I told Victor that I thought we were
all traveling heavy with illusions.

I kept trying to write this voice-over without using the last line. I didn't think it worked, but David Skinner, the executive producer, was convinced it did work. Of course, it's a beautiful moment and I was completely wrong.

◆ *Scenes* 90–96: These scenes were cut from the film for various reasons. The good-bye scenes were cut because they felt too much like "the end" of the film. The humorous scenes were cut because they contrasted too sharply with the powerful scenes of Victor cutting his hair in the trailer. We wanted to move directly from the trailer in Scene 88 to the argument between Victor and Thomas in the pickup in Scene 97. We also cut these scenes because Victor's wig is so bad and we wanted to hide it for as long as possible.

LESSON LEARNED: If you want to butcher a wig properly, let a gaffer or grip do the cutting.

✦ *Scenes 98–116*: When Chris shot scenes from the car wreck at the Sundance Institute, they were surreal, original, and scary as hell. But he chose to shoot them in a much more realistic fashion here. As a result, the oddness of the wreck (the storytelling, the dead dog, etc.) played very flatly. In the end, these scenes simply took too long to happen. They were cut down to the bare bones.

Brian Berdan is responsible for the editing during Victor's run. He decided that Suzy Song's voice and image should be a part of the scene. This went a long way toward establishing the mystery and magic of Suzy and, combined with the house fire imagery, foreshadowed Suzy's burning of Arnold's trailer in Phoenix. Brian also suggested that a small part of Arnold Joseph's Jesuit basketball monologue should be placed here as well.

LESSON LEARNED: The film editor is a director and a screenwriter.

✦ *Scene 118*: We cut a lot of the dialogue in this scene because it was unnecessary exposition. We also reversed the order of the scene so that the "Tonto and Tonto" joke came first, to relieve the tension of the car wreck and run.

✦ *Scene 119*: Most of this was cut from the film because it was repetitious and not as funny as it read on the page. We used the end of the scene where Thomas pushed Victor into the room where the Police Chief was waiting.

✦ *Scene 120*: We cut a lot of dialogue from this scene in order to create more silence and add to the tension.

At the end of this scene, Tom Skerritt improvised by gently twisting the lid of Arnold's ash can and then pulling his hand away in disgust when Victor revealed what was inside the can. A very funny moment.

✦ *Scenes 122–123:* There is dialogue that sounds wise and wonderful when it's on the page, but merely sounds pretentious and forced when seen on the screen. This scene was filled with that kind of dialogue. We cut this scene extensively in order to focus on the moment where Victor apologizes to Thomas. That was what the scene was about anyway, not the endless exchange of items. This is another example of overwriting the screenplay, which is, I suppose, better than underwriting it. I mean, we can always cut the overwrites, enit?

✦ *Scenes 124–129:* Chris and I disagreed about the focus of this series of scenes. As written, Suzy sets the trailer on fire and that also starts the pickup afire. As edited by Chris, the pickup starts and also ignites the trailer fire. In the end, we cut it as written. Suzy is a powerful and mysterious Indian woman who literally and symbolically "frees" Arnold from his Arizona grave by burning his trailer down. A bad fire destroyed Arnold's life. A good fire redeems him.

Note on music: Jim Boyd and I wrote the song that plays here, "Father and Farther," many years before this movie, but it perfectly fits the theme.

✦ *Scenes 130–132:* All of these were cut because they were too domestic. We let the mystery be.

✦ *Scene 135:* Cut from the film for pacing reasons.

✦ *Scene 141:* Though Chris and the producers wanted to keep it, I cut most of the dialogue in this scene. I wanted the scene to focus on Victor's decision to not tell Thomas the truth about the house fire that killed his parents. That is, by far, the greatest gift Victor could give Thomas.

✦ *Scenes 142–145:* The Disc Jockey and Lester were moved to the beginning of the film. We didn't need them here. We were rapidly heading toward resolution and the humor just got in the way of that.

✦ *Scene 147:* We cut all of the dialogue out of this scene and played it silently. One, because the humor was inappropriate, and two, because we have no idea what Arlene Joseph is thinking at this moment. I didn't think it was up to me or Chris or anybody else to decide what she would say here. I wanted to give her that much respect.

✦ *Scene 148:* Velma and Lucy are cut from the film here because we didn't need the humor, though these cut scenes are probably the funniest we shot.

✦ *Scene 149:* Not shot.

✦ *Scene 151:* The ending of this film caused the biggest conflict between Chris and me. First of all, we didn't have the time or money to put all of those Indians on the shores of the river, and we certainly didn't have the money to create a computer graphics image of a salmon leaping from the water. But Chris chose to have only the Young Victor and Young Thomas standing onshore when Arnold rose from the river. This, of course, was completely opposite of what I intended with the screenplay. I wanted Arnold to rise and return to his entire family, not just the boys. I mean, Arnold had already abandoned the women in his life and, in Chris's version of the ending, was abandoning them yet again.

In any case, we gathered all of the cast and appropriate crew and reshot the ending a few weeks after we wrapped. We reshot it as written in the screenplay and I discovered I didn't like my ending either. In fact, I disliked my ending more than I disliked Chris's version.

During test screenings, Chris was arguing for his version but I knew neither his ending nor mine was going to work. They were both too sentimental and predictable.

I didn't know what to do. But then I decided that we could reverse the whole sequence. So, with Brian Berdan's expert editing, I began the scene at the source of the river and moved downstream to the bridge where Victor throws his father's ashes into the water. Instead of a "happy ending" we now have an ending that's much more poetic, much more emotional, much more unpredictable and open-ended.

MIRAMAX FILMS *Presents*

A SHADOWCATCHER ENTERTAINMENT *Production*

in Association with SHERMAN ALEXIE

a Film by CHRIS EYRE

S M O K E   S I G N A L S

Directed by
CHRIS EYRE

Screenplay by
SHERMAN ALEXIE
Based on stories from his book
The Lone Ranger and Tonto Fistfight in Heaven

Produced by
LARRY ESTES
and
SCOTT ROSENFELT

Executive Producers
DAVID SKINNER
CARL BRESSLER

Co-producers
SHERMAN ALEXIE
CHRIS EYRE

Starring

ADAM BEACH

EVAN ADAMS

IRENE BEDARD

GARY FARMER

TANTOO CARDINAL

CODY LIGHTNING
MICHELLE ST. JOHN

ROBERT MIANO
MOLLY CHEEK

SIMON BAKER
MONIQUE MOJICA

ELAINE MILES
MICHAEL GREYEYES

LEONARD GEORGE
JOHN TRUDELL
DARWIN HAINE

with TOM SKERRITT

CYNTHIA GEARY

and PERREY REEVES

Casting by COREEN MAYRS

Director of Photography
BRIAN CAPENER

Production Designer
CHARLES ARMSTRONG

Costume Designer
RON LEAMON

Edited by
BRIAN BERDAN

Music by
BC SMITH

Associate Producers
ROGER BAERWOLF
RANDY SUHR

Line Producer
BRENT MORRIS

Victor Joseph	ADAM BEACH
Thomas Builds-the-Fire	EVAN ADAMS
Suzy Song	IRENE BEDARD
Arnold Joseph	GARY FARMER
Arlene Joseph	TANTOO CARDINAL

Young Victor Joseph	CODY LIGHTNING
Young Thomas Builds-the-Fire	SIMON BAKER
Grandma Builds-the-Fire	MONIQUE MOJICA
Randy Peone	JOHN TRUDELL
Lester Fallsapart	LEONARD GEORGE
Junior Polatkin	MICHAEL GREYEYES
Boo	DARWIN HAINE
Velma	MICHELLE ST. JOHN
Lucy	ELAINE MILES
Cathy the Gymnast	CYNTHIA GEARY
Cowboy	GARY TAYLOR
Holly	PERREY REEVES
Julie	NICOLETTE VAJTAY
Penny	MOLLY CHEEK
Burt	ROBERT MIANO
Police Chief	TOM SKERRITT
Jesuit #1	TODD JAMIESON
Stunt Coordinator	RON OTIS, A-1 STUNTS
Stunt Player	ART HICKMAN

Developed with the Assistance of
THE SUNDANCE INSTITUTE

Unit Production Manager	ANTHONY VOZZA
First Assistant Director	JO SHILLING
Director's Assistant	HEIDI MCGOWEN
2nd Second Assistant Director	MEGAN MURPHY
Los Angeles Casting	ANYA COLLOFF
Seattle Casting	JODI ROTHFIELD
Casting Associate to Coreen Mayrs	HEIKE BRANDSTATTER
1st Assistant Camera	LARRY WRIGHT
2nd Assistant Camera	WILLIAM CRESS
Steadicam Operator	ROBIN BUERKI
Camera Loader	STEPHEN MACDOUGALL
Art Director	JONATHON SATUREN
Set Decorator	DAWN FERRY
Property Master	MELISSA MATTHIES
Prop Assistant	DAVID BOWEN
Storyboard Artist	AIDAN HUGHES
Key Make-up Artist	CYNTHIA BORNIA
Assistant Hair and Make-up Artist	NADIA FELKER
Wardrobe Supervisor	EARL LEWIS
Additional Seamstress	BERTHA SWAN

Script Supervisor	JANET FRIES ECKHOLM
Production Sound Mixer	DOUGLAS TOURTELOT, C.A.S.
Boom Operator	STEVE WILLER
Location Manager	SHAUN SULLIVAN
Production Coordinator	KRISTEN CORNING
Set Production Coordinator	TODD GLINSMAN
Assistant Production Coordinator	CARA MIA HARRIS
Key Set Production Assistant	PETER JENSEN
Special Effects Coordinator	RAY BROWN
Assistant Special Effects	ROBERT "SMOKEY" SIMOKOVIC
Additional Effects	JOEL YOUNGERMAN
Gaffer	PAT SHELLENBERGER
Best Boy Electric	ERIC MOORE
Electricians	ANDREW WALLACE
	SOMSY VEJSIRI
	ERIK LOYSEN
	CHRIS KOVALSKI
	KATY BURBANK
	ERIC BLACKERBY
	PETE JOHNSON
	DAN BAHEZA
	STEVE COLGROVE
Key Grip	KRIST HAGER
Best Boy Grip	SIERRA MORGAN
Dolly Grip	DAVID DARROW
Grips	CRAIG BILODEAU
	DAN PETERS
	VERN PETERS
	BEN KENYON
	LANCE O'DELL
	JOHN EAMES
	MATT CLARK
Unit Still Photographers	JILL SABELLA
	COURTNAY DUCHIN
Second Unit Director	RANDY SUHR
Second Unit Director of Photography	PAUL MAILMAN
Second Unit First Camera Assistant	DAVID LEYSE
Post Production Supervisor	JANET FRIES ECKHOLM
Assistant Editor	JOHN HELDE
Music Supervisor	BC SMITH
Music Conductor and Orchestrator	TIM SIMONEC
Orchestra Contractor	SIMON JAMES
Associate Music Supervisor	CHRIS MOCK

Music Mixer	RICK WINQUEST
Music Engineers	DIMITRI JAKIMOWICS
	DON GILMORE
Synth Programming and Design	ZACK BELICA AND CHRIS MOCK
Assistant Music Engineers	SAM HOFSTEDT
	JOHN BURTON
Re-Recording Mixers	JAMES WILLIAMS
	JOHN BRASHER, C.A.S.
	MARTY HUTCHERSON
	ERIC HOESCHEN
	MIKE MINKLER
	FRANK MONTANO
Sound Design	PATRICK O'SULLIVAN
SFX Editors	DAVID BACH
	PEGGY MCAFFEE
ADR Supervisor	SARAH BRADY, M.P.S.E.
ADR Mixer	BRIAN SMITH
ADR Editor	NANCY LEE BLEISCH
ADR Assistant	MARGIE LALA
Dialogue Editor	BRUCE MURPHY
Dialogue Assistant	LAURENCE PUCHALSKY
Foley Artist	MONIQUE REYMOND
ADR and Foley Mixer	ERIC HOESCHEN
Sound Editors	JOE MILNER
	NANCY MACLEOD
Assistant Sound Editor	SCOTT TAYLOR
Post Sound Recordists	CARLOS ISAIS
	STEVE KOHLER
Engineer	RICK MACLANE
Loader	CHRIS SPARKES
Sound Supervisor	PAUL TIMOTHY CARDEN
Sound Services Managers	MIMI STARRETT
	GEOFF CLARK
Production Accountant	CYNTHIA WALKER
First Assistant Accountant	LAURA AUSTER
Post Production Accountants	PETER JENSEN
	DEBORAH RATHBONE
Office Managers	KATHY KOZU
	LIZA COMTOIS
Office Production Assistant	CRISTINE REYNOLDS
Office Intern	TIFFANY CRAWFORD
Studio Teacher	HARLEY GOODBEAR
Extras Casting	HEATHER RAE
Stand-ins	BILLY TONASKET
	HEATHER KAY
	GARY MOFFITT

Transportation Coordinator	BART HEIMBURGER
Transportation Captain	DAN FISHER
Bus Driver	CHUCK HOWARD
Drivers	MOLLY LITTLE
	BRENDON MCKEON
	JOE SOLEBURG
	BILL POWELL
	RON KING
	JOHN WOLFE
	CLINT YOAKUM
	CYNTHIA WILLIAMS
	VERN JOHNSON
	DIANE EVE
Helicopter Operator	JOHN SCANLON
	RIVER CITY HELICOPTERS
Caterers	PREMIERE CATERING
	ADAM MORRISON
	JUSTIN CRAPO
Idaho Craft Service	INEZ SIJOHN
	BINGO SIJOHN
Washington Craft Service	ALEXANDRA BURESH
Filmed with	PANAVISION® CAMERAS AND LENSES
Additional Camera Equipment	OPPENHEIMER CAMERA
Grip and Electric Equipment	FILMLITES LTD.
Additional Grip Equipment	NORTH BY NORTHWEST PRODUCTIONS
Crane	JONAS JENSEN STUDIOS, INC.
Idaho Construction	RED BIRD CONSTRUCTION
Washington Construction	ST. MARIE CONSTRUCTION
Picture Car	EVERGREEN STAGE LINE, INC.
Production Vehicles	BUDGET RENT-A-TRUCK
	THRIFTY CAR RENTAL
	ENTERPRISE LEASING CO.
On Set Medics	POST FALLS AMBULANCE & RESCUE
	EPHRATA AMBULANCE SERVICE
Fire Safety	GRANT COUNTY FIRE DEPT.
	PLUMMER FIRE DEPARTMENT
Payroll	MEDIA SERVICES
Banking Services	UNION BANK OF CALIFORNIA
	U.S. BANK OF WASHINGTON
Insurance	AON/ALBERT G. RUBEN
Legal Services	LICHTER, GROSSMAN, NICHOLS & ADLER, INC.

Clearances	JOAN PEARCE RESEARCH ASSOCIATES
Publicity	BAKER • WINOKUR • RYDER
Film Stock	EASTMAN KODAK
Film Stock Supplied by	REEL GOOD, INC.
Product Placement	MOTION PICTURE MAGIC, INC.
	CREATIVE ENTERTAINMENT SERVICES, INC.
	UPP ENTERTAINMENT MARKETING
	PREMIER ENTERTAINMENT SERVICES
Security	EASTERN WASHINGTON SECURITY
	SECURITY MANAGEMENT
Film Laboratory	ALPHA CINE LABS, INC.
Color Timer and Film Lab Manager	BILL SCOTT
Video Dailies	RAY SMITHWICK
Lab Coordinators	KIM SHERWOOD
	ROBERTA UKURA
Negative Cutters	ANDY PRATT
	STEPHEN LES
Titles and Opticals Production	PACIFIC TITLE
Titles and Opticals Lab	HOLLYWOOD FILM AND VIDEO
Digital Transfer	DIGITAL DEVOID
Optical Sound Track	N.T. AUDIO
Editing Services and Facilities	STRAIGHT CUT, SEATTLE
Music Recording and Mixing Facility	STUDIO X, SEATTLE
Post Production Sound Facilities	BRASHER SOUND
	BUENA VISTA SOUND
Looping Group	SMALL TALK
Players	EDWIN COOK
	GREGORY NORMAN CRUZ
	WENDY HOFFMAN
	MICHAEL HORSE
	SANDRA HORSE

COMPOSED MUSIC

Native American Drums and Vocals	VAUGHN EAGLEBEAR
	FERDINAND LOUIE
	AARON "SCARBO" MARCHAND

	ANDRÉ L. PICARD, JR.
	PETE SEMOE
	JOHN SIROIS
	PATRICK WATT
Orchestra	NORTHWEST SINFONIA
Special Vocals Performance	ULALI
Producer of Special Vocals	DAVID BEAL
Special Vocals Recorded and Mixed by	TOM CASSEL AND DAVID BEAL
Electric Guitars	DUDLEY TAFT
	DAVE PETERSON
Electric Bass	BRAD HOUSER
	CHUCK DEARDORF
Vocals	KRISTEN OWEN
	RON RAY AND DIONNA LONG
	OF THE BAND "HIT EXPLOSION"
Drums and Taos Drums	BEN SMITH
	STEVE HILL

SONGS

"HER SONG"
Music and Lyrics by André L. Picard, Jr.
Performed by André L. Picard, Jr.
and John Sirois

"TREATIES"
Music by Jim Boyd
Lyrics by Sherman Alexie
Performed by Jim Boyd and
Debra, Pam and Lori Ludwig
Courtesy of Thunderwolf Records

"RESERVATION BLUES"
Written and Performed by Jim Boyd
Lyrics by Sherman Alexie
Courtesy of Thunderwolf Records

"ROAD BUDDY"
Written and Performed by Dar Williams
Copyright Burning Field Music
Administered by Bug Music, Inc. (ASCAP)
Dar Williams Appears Courtesy of
Razor & Tie Entertainment, LLC.

"A MILLION MILES AWAY"
Written and Performed by Jim Boyd
Lyrics by Sherman Alexie
Courtesy of Thunderwolf Records

"ALL MY RELATIONS"
Music by Garry Owen
Lyrics by Pura Fe
Performed by ULALI
(Pura Fe, Soni Moreno, Jennifer Kreisberg)
Produced by ULALI and David Beal
Pura Fe Appears Courtesy of
Shanachie Records
Copyright Corn, Beans and Squash Music
(ASCAP)

"JOHN WAYNE'S TEETH"
Written and Performed by Eaglebear Singers
Lyrics by Sherman Alexie

"FATHER AND FARTHER"
Written and Performed by Jim Boyd
Lyrics by Sherman Alexie
Courtesy of Thunderwolf Records

"WAHJEELEH-YIHM"
Written and Performed by ULALI
(Pura Fe, Soni Moreno, Jennifer Kreisberg)
Produced by David Beal
Recorded at Noise Productions, Inc.
Pura Fe Appears Courtesy of
Shanachie Records
Copyright Corn, Beans and Squash Music
(ASCAP)

THANKS TO THE FOLLOWING

Morgan Entrekin   Allen Daviau

Brad Bond and Diane Bracey   Rick Pagano and Debi Manwiller

Rindy and Steve Dallas   Peter Masterson and Carlin Glynn

Tim Craig   Nancy Stauffer

Judy Hottensen   Sally Jo Effenson

Mark Long   Susan Grode

Leo Rossi   Andy Wolk

Wray Wade   Eric Price

Adam Moos   Ava Hamilton

Jacqueline Milles   Cindy Stillwell

Miwa Messer   René Haynes

Susan Muir   Nelson George

Jeremiah Newton   Patricia Hilden

Elizabeth Schmitz   L.M. "Kit" Carson

Jadina Lilien   Tailinh Prado

Robert Hershon   Wesley Strick

Boris Fruman   Ben Dupris

Mark Pawlak   Donna Brook

Lori Pourier   Paul Mezey

Ron Schreiber   Alex Kuo

Mary Bowannie   Jon Kilik

Dean Curtis Bear Claw   Bob Johnson and Jim Gulian

Chris Roberts   Daniel Melnick

Shazz Bennett   Craig McKay

Rachel Chanoff   Rose Anderson

Alice Arlen   Gretchen Huizinga

Kathleen McGinnis   Holly Becker

Tyler McKenzie   Cochise Anderson

Gil Silverbird   Steven LeBret

Susan Harmon   Ann Wilson

Mindee Nodvin

Native American Producers Alliance
The Advisors and Staff of the Sundance Filmmakers Lab
Art Matters Foundation
The Rockefeller Foundation Intercultural Film Fellowship
Rutherford Productions
Baron & Baron Studios
Reed Ruddy and Studio X
Lila Wallace—Reader's Digest Writers' Award
Suzy Kellett and the Washington State Film Office
Donna James and the City of Seattle Film Office

Thomas Builds-the-Fire's End Monologue
is adapted from the poem "Forgiving Our Fathers" by Dick Lourie
Courtesy of Hanging Loose Press

THE PRODUCERS GRATEFULLY ACKNOWLEDGE AND EXTEND SPECIAL THANKS TO THE FOLLOWING

The SiJohn Family and The Coeur d'Alene Tribe
Ernie Stensgar, Coeur d'Alene Tribal Chairman
The Coeur d'Alene Tribal Council

The Residents and Cities of
Coeur d'Alene, DeSmet, Plummer, Tensed and Worley, Idaho
Spokane and Soap Lake, Washington

Kelly Simpson and The Panavision New Filmmaker Program
Pat Doyle and Pacific Title
Alex Moradian and Hollywood Film and Video
Maggie Considine and Blake Himm, Taos Drums
David Beal and Noise Productions, Inc.

Sharon Bialy   Michelle Satter
Lynn Auerbach   Jane Jenkins
Maricel Pagulayan Janet Hirshenson
Montana Artists   Michael Hirshenson
Randy Gaiber   Bettie Roecks

Coca-Cola Enterprises
Casio, Inc.
JanSport, Inc.

Minolta Corporation
Nora Beverages
Nortel
RAM Sports, Inc.

FILMED ON LOCATION
on the Coeur d'Alene Indian Reservation, Idaho
in DeSmet, Plummer, Tensed and Worley, Idaho
and Spokane and Soap Lake, Washington

Produced with the support
of the Cinema 100 / Sundance International Award
sponsored by NHK, NHK Enterprises 21 Inc., The Seiyu, Ltd.,
Kinema Junpo and the Sundance Institute

Support HONOR THE EARTH Campaign
Support the AMERICAN INDIAN COLLEGE FUND
Contributions from the profits of this film
will be made to each of these Organizations